Claude Monet 1908

'THINGS OF BEAUTY'

WHAT TWO SISTERS DID FOR WALES

First published in 2007 by National Museum Wales Books,
Cathays Park, Cardiff, CF10 3NP, Wales.
Reprinted in 2009.

ISBN 978 0 7200 0581 3

Production: Mari Gordon
Design: mopublications.com
Printed by: Gomer Press
Available in Welsh as *Cyfoeth, celf a chydwybod: llafur cariad chwiorydd Gregynog*
ISBN 978 0 7200 0582 0

Front cover: Margaret Davies, photographed in her mid-twenties. *Private collection.*

Inside front cover: Gwendoline Davies, photographed in 1937. *Private collection.*

Fly leaf: Claude Monet, *Waterlilies*, (1908)

Half title page: Gregynog Hall today. *Ray Edgar*

Back cover: Camille Pissarro, *Sunset, Port of Rouen*, 1898. Margaret bought this painting in 1920.
She knew Rouen from her time there in 1919. Perhaps the view of industrial shipping also appealed to her,
as a reminder of how her grandfather founded the family's wealth by mining and transporting coal
across the world in the Industrial Revolution.

In 1918, Margaret and Gwendoline Davies funded a project close to their hearts, the formation of an Arts and
Crafts Museum as part of the University of Wales. The Museum's collection, according to the drawing master
Dan Jones, used '**Things of beauty**' in order to 'instruct and inspire for the welfare of the coming generations'.
This book explores the full range of the sisters' commitment to achieving this.

'THINGS OF BEAUTY'

WHAT TWO SISTERS DID FOR WALES

Edited by
Oliver Fairclough

NATIONAL MUSEUM WALES BOOKS 2007

PREFACE

Amgueddfa Cymru – National Museum Wales celebrates its centenary with this book and the exhibition it complements. They both give new insights into the lives and characters of two remarkable but very private women who were the greatest benefactors of the Museum's first hundred years. They are Gwendoline and Margaret Davies – pioneer collectors of Impressionist and Post-Impressionist art – from Llandinam in Montgomeryshire. Their bequests in 1951 and 1963 utterly transformed the range and quality of Wales's national art collection.

The sisters' values, shared with the liberal non-conformist elite of early twentieth-century Wales, meant that their art collection encapsulated the cultural aspirations of Wales at that time. This book can only hint at the range and scale of their philanthropy and that of their brother David. However, there are still visible legacies of the family's generosity in many parts of Wales today. In Cardiff, the National Museum and the Temple of Peace; in Aberystwyth, the Edward Davies Building at the University College, now the School of Art, and the National Library with its Gregynog Gallery; and elsewhere the numerous chapels, hospitals, halls and playing fields (and many others that are now gone – like the pits from which the family originally drew their wealth). Then there is Oriel Davies in Newtown, with its exceptional exhibition and education programme. Above all, there is Gregynog, 'unique among country houses in Wales' and the sisters' home for much of their lives. Margaret bequeathed it to the University of Wales, and it is now a thriving residential conference centre.

Despite this legacy, the sisters' endeavours to improve the well-being of their countrymen through art, music and the discussion of social problems, astonishing in their idealism and as relevant now as in the 1930s, remain too little-known. Known to family and friends as Gwen and Daisy, the sisters never married and were sometimes perceived as shy and ill-at-ease in company. Gentle and in some ways rather sad figures in their middle age, they were burdened by the responsibility of having great wealth amid poverty and suffering and by their religious obligation to use that wealth to benefit others as well as themselves. Margaret was sometimes found removing coal from the fire if she felt it had been piled extravagantly, and it was said in the family that 'it was always easier to get £10,000 out of Aunt Daisy than half-a-crown.'

Right: Margaret Sidney Davies (1884-1963) and Gwendoline Elizabeth Davies (1882-1951).

A visit to Gregynog in the 1920s and 1930s was perhaps not always unalloyed enjoyment. Their cousin, George Maitland Lloyd Davies, briefly Christian Pacifist MP for the University of Wales, once wrote of 'the horrors of Gregynog', and others found the great house, which cost the then astonishing sum of £10,000 a year to run, somewhat daunting. Gatherings there were strictly teetotal – although the sisters were once persuaded that a supply of alcoholic beverages should be ordered from Harrod's for the Prime Minister Stanley Baldwin. The atmosphere at Gregynog was generally cool and correct and guests were expected to attend the non-denominational act of worship that took place on Sundays. Nevertheless, most visitors were bowled over by the wonderful music, the richness of the art and the beauty of the gardens, as well as by the sisters' simplicity and utter sincerity. Three-quarters of a century later, it can be hard to get beyond a public image of the sisters as the chatelaines of Gregynog. This book presents a different and happier picture of them as young women before the First World War, when they began to collect Impressionist art, as well as exploring the devastating impact the War had on them. Their fundamental goodness and extraordinary achievements also shine through every chapter. As one visitor to Gregynog wrote, 'it was a case of unlimited means, being wisely and very well spent'.

This is the first extended study of the sisters since Eirene White's *The Ladies of Gregynog* of 1985, which was based on the author's personal knowledge and memories. We hope that we have complemented this, and that this book will stimulate further work on these two women, who did so much for Wales and its people.

Michael Houlihan

Director General
Amgueddfa Cymru – National Museum Wales

ACKNOWLEDGEMENTS

Because Gwendoline and Margaret Davies's philanthropy touched so many areas of Welsh life, an exceptionally large number of people have been generous with time and information. First among these is the sisters' great nephew, David, the present Lord Davies of Llandinam, and his wife Bea. This book is largely based on the family papers and photographs in their care, and would have been quite impossible without their kindness in making these available and their patience in replying to a bewildering range of questions. The sisters' niece Jean Cormack and their cousin Elizabeth Rowlands-Hughes shared personal memories of them, and we are also very grateful for information from Camilla Davies. Professor Ian Parrott, Ottoline Mary Jones, Thelma Watkin, Margaret Doreen Shuker, Clive Edwards and Gwyneth Williams all allowed us to record their memories of life at Gregynog. Robert Blayney, John Christopher, Graham Richards, Brian Taylor, A. J. Heward Rees and Jayne Davies wrote to us about their experiences of the sisters and of Gregynog. From Australia, Mary Hackett sent us copies of her letters describing her 'Welsh adventure' in the summer of 1938. David Lewis was also hugely generous with his own research on Gregynog and the Press.

We would like to thank Wendy Butler (UCL Records Office); Dr Rhian Davies; Dr Susan J. Davies (Department of History & Welsh History, University of Wales, Aberystwyth); Mark Evans (Victoria and Albert Museum); Lindsay Evans; Amanda Farr and Clare Martin at Oriel Davies, Newtown; Andrew Green and his staff at Llyfrgell Genedlaethol Cymru: The National Library of Wales; Dorothy Harrop; Hugh Herbert Jones; Neil Holland (School of Art, University of Wales, Aberystwyth); Dr Glyn Tegai Hughes (formerly Warden of Gregynog); Ben Jones; Dr Susan Jones (Director of Gregynog); Ruth Lambert; Dr Margaret McCance; Susan Morgan; Mary Oldham (Librarian at Gregynog); Rowan O'Neill (BBC Cymru Wales); Dafydd Rowlands-Hughes; Carolyn Stewart; Paul Islwyn Thomas (Indus Films); David Vickers (Gwasg Gregynog) and Yasmine Webb (Barnet Local Studies and Archives) for all their help and support.

We owe a special debt to Professor Prys Morgan, who wrote the introduction, and who shared his own memories of Greygynog in the 1960s, and Robert Meyrick, who contributed the chapter on life at Gregynog and whose knowledge of the Davies sisters and their adviser Hugh Blaker is encyclopaedic.

At the Museum, the authors are grateful for the support of Andrew Renton, Beth McIntyre, Charlotte Topsfield, Tim Egan and Clare Smith (all of the Department of Art). New photographs were taken and other images were digitised by the Photography Department, and information was supplied by Ceri Thompson (Curator of Coal, Big Pit) and Linda Norton (Cartographer, Geology). Production was by Mari Gordon (Publications Department).

The work has been kept on track by Melanie Youngs, who as part-time administrator of the project was also its conscience. The exhibition was made possible by a grant from the Gwendoline and Margaret Davies charities which, like their founders, have long been outstandingly generous supporters of the Museum.

Right: Jean-François Millet, *The Peasant Family*, 1871-2. Margaret Davies bought this unfinished work, by one of her favourite artists, in 1911. It depicts a Norman peasant family in their farmyard.

CONTENTS

WHO WAS WHO IN THE WORLD
OF THE DAVIES SISTERS

Baldwin, Stanley
(1867-1947), 1st Earl
Baldwin of Bewdley:
industrialist; Conservative
politician; Prime Minister
1923, 1924-29, 1935-7;
visited Gregynog for a
recuperative holiday in
August and September 1936.

Baxandall, David Kighley
(1905-1992): curator;
assistant keeper of Art,
National Museum of Wales
1929-39, keeper 1939-41;
director, Manchester City Art
Galleries 1945-52; director,
National Galleries of Scotland
1952-9.

Blaker, Hugh
(1873-1936): artist; collector;
dealer; curator, Holburne
Museum of Art, Bath;
adviser on art purchases to
Gwendoline and Margaret.

Blaker, Jane
(1869-1947): sister of Hugh
Blaker; governess and later
companion to Gwendoline
and Margaret and to their
stepmother.

Boult, Sir Adrian
(1889-1983): conductor;
regularly conducted at
Gregynog and
Montgomeryshire County
Music Festivals; conductor of
the BBC Symphony
Orchestra, 1931-50.

Bray, Horace Walter
(1877-1963): worked with
R. A. Maynard as a wood-
engraver at the Gregynog
Press.

Davies, David
(1818-1890): variously
nicknamed 'Top Sawyer', a
reference to his early days in
Montgomeryshire sawpits, or
'Davies the Ocean', after his
Ocean Coal company;
founder of the family fortune;
civil engineering and railway
contractor; pioneer of the coal
industry; chief promoter of
Barry docks; MP; patron of
religious and educational
causes; Gwendoline and
Margaret's grandfather.

Davies, Margaret
(1814-1894, née Jones):
David Davies's wife. From

Y Wern, Llanfair Caereinion,
he met her while building
Neuadd bridge over the River
Banwy in 1852; Gwendoline
and Margaret's grandmother.

Davies, Edward
(1852-1898): only child of
David and Margaret Davies;
industrialist; Gwendoline and
Margaret's father.

Davies, Mary
(1850-1888, née Jones):
Edward Davies's first wife:
from Llwynderw, Llandinam;
Gwendoline and Margaret's
mother.

Davies, Elizabeth
(1853-1942, née Jones):
younger sister of Mary
Davies; Edward Davies's second wife; from Llwynderw,
Llandinam; Gwendoline and
Margaret's stepmother.

Davies, David
(1880-1944), 1st Lord Davies
of Llandinam: son of
Edward and Mary Davies;
industrialist; philanthropist;
MP; promoter of the League
of Nations; elder brother of

Gwendoline and Margaret.

Davies, David
(1915-1944): 2nd Lord Davies of Llandinam, known as 'Mike'; son of David, 1st Lord Davies and Amy Davies, née Penman; died of wounds sustained in action in Holland, September 1944; nephew to Gwendoline and Margaret.

Davies, David
(b.1940): 3rd Lord Davies of Llandinam; son of David, 2nd Lord Davies of Llandinam and Eldrydd Davies, née Dugdale; great-nephew of Gwendoline and Margaret.

Davies, Sir Henry Walford
(1869-1941): composer; first Gregynog Professor of Music, University College of Wales, Aberystwyth; Chair of the National Council of Music; Master of the King's Musick (1934-41); musical adviser and confidant to Gwendoline.

Evans, Thomas
(?-1943): managing director, Ocean, Wilson & Co. Ltd in the inter-war years.

Fisher, George
(1879-1970): bookbinder to the Gregynog Press.

Fleure, Herbert John
(1877-1969): anthropologist and geographer; Gregynog Professor of Geography at the University College of Wales, Aberystwyth, 1917-30.

Greenslade, Sidney Kyffin
(1866-1955): architect; designer of the main block of the National Library of Wales, Aberystwyth; consulting curator of the Arts & Crafts

Above: The Prime Minister, Stanley Baldwin, talking to Elizabeth Davies after the tree-planting ceremony in August 1936 (see page 105).

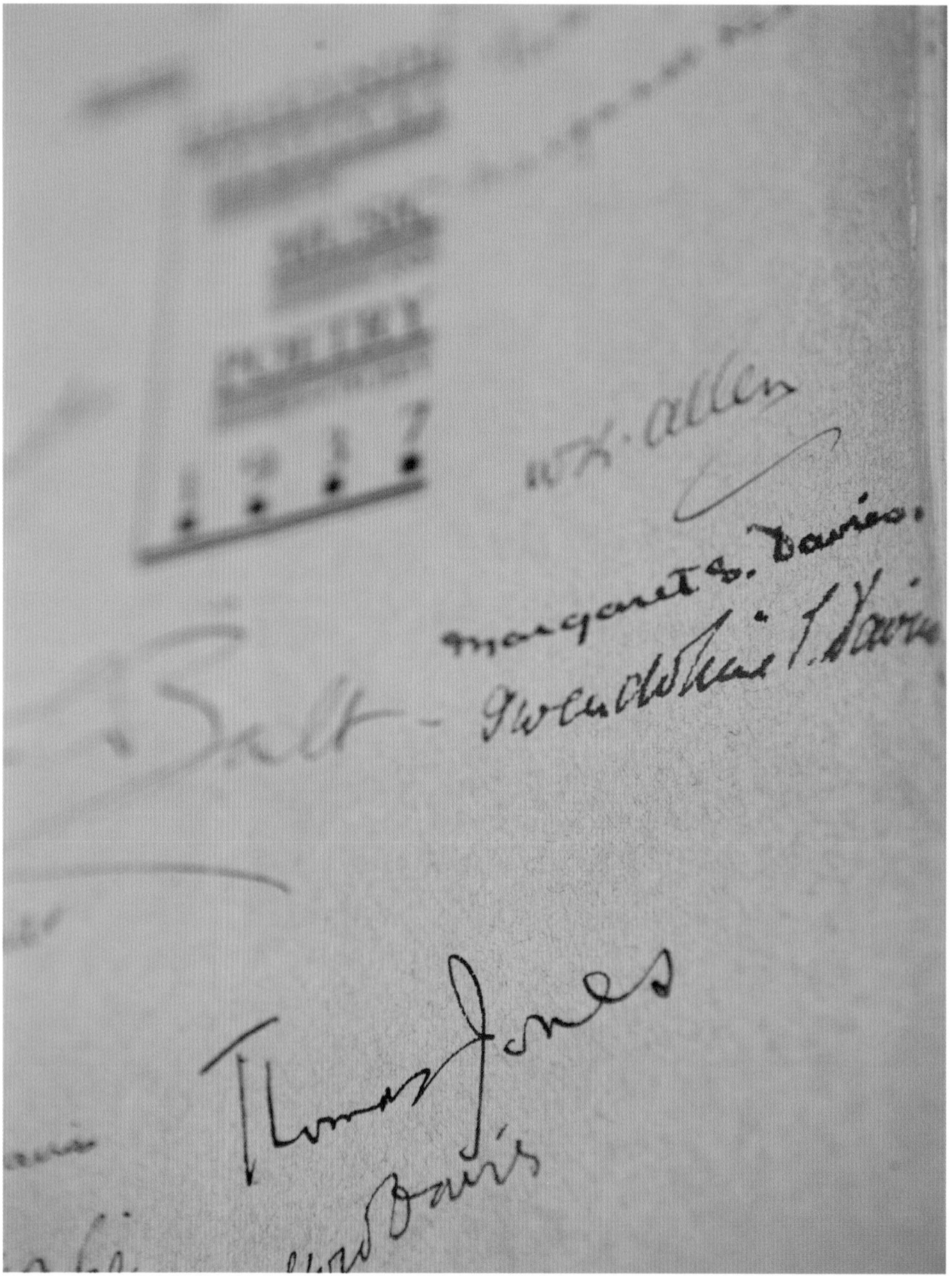
Margaret S. Davies.
Thomas Jones

Museum at the University College of Wales, Aberystwyth.

Haberly, Loyd
(1896-1981): poet and printer; third Controller of the Gregynog Press.

Hermes, Gertrude
(1901-1983): sculptor and print-maker; wood-engraver at the Gregynog Press; wife of Blair Hughes-Stanton.

Holst, Gustav
(1874-1934): composer; taught at St Paul's School, Hammersmith from 1905; attended 1933 Gregynog Festival, later writing *O Spiritual Pilgrim* for the Gregynog Choir.

Hughes-Stanton, Blair
(1902-1981): wood-engraver and designer of bindings; colleague of William McCance at the Gregynog Press; husband of Gertrude Hermes.

Jenkins, William
(?-1929): first general manager of the Ocean collieries.

Jones, Dora Herbert
(1890-1974, née Rowlands): secretary to the Gregynog Press; pioneer of Welsh folk music; friend and confidante to the sisters.

Jones, Thomas
(1870-1955 known as 'T.J.'): civil servant and educationalist; Deputy Secretary to the Cabinet, 1916-30; chairman of the Gregynog Press Board; founder of Coleg Harlech; secretary of the Pilgrim Trust; adviser to, and confidant of, Gwendoline and Margaret.

Maynard, Robert Ashwin
(1888-1966): artist; first Controller of the Gregynog Press.

McCance, William
(1894-1970): artist; second Controller of the Gregynog Press; husband of Agnes Miller Parker.

Parker, Agnes Miller
(1895-1980): wood-engraver for the Gregynog Press; wife of William McCance.

Parrott, Professor Ian
(b.1916), composer, teacher,

author; Gregynog Professor of Music, University College of Wales, Aberystwyth 1954-83; Gregynog Festival organizer, 1955-61; author of *The Spiritual Pilgrims*, which details the Davies sisters' musical lives.

Steegman, John Edward Horatio
(1899-1966): art and drama critic; curator, National Portrait Gallery 1926-45; keeper of Art, National Museum of Wales, 1945-52, director, Museum of Fine Arts, Montreal, 1952-9.

Thomson, David Croal
(1855-1930): art dealer; admirer of Corot and Whistler; adviser on art purchases to Gwendoline and Margaret.

Urquhart, Murray
(1882-1972): painter; friend and adviser on art to Gwendoline and Margaret.

Wardrop, James
(1905-1957): printer; fourth and last Controller of the Gregynog Press, while also remaining on the staff of the National Art Library at the Victoria and Albert Museum.

Left: The 1937 Gregynog Festival programme, signed by Gwendoline and Margaret Davies, Thomas Jones, Sir Walford Davies, Sir Adrian Boult and others. *Ray Edgar*

INTRODUCTION:
THE WORLD OF THE DAVIES FAMILY

The sisters Margaret and Gwendoline Davies led 'two quiet lives' according to their friend Eirene White, but the Wales in which they lived was one of great stress and strain. Welsh capitalism, of which the Davies dynasty was a vital component, was building up to a crisis in industrial relations in 1910, although the Davies's own port of Barry was about to overtake Cardiff in 1913 as the greatest coal-exporting port in the world. Welsh nonconformity, of which the Davies family formed part of the elite of Calvinist families, had undergone great convulsions in the Revival of 1904-5. Welsh Liberalism seemed to reach its greatest heights after the 1906 election, especially during Lloyd George's premiership from 1916 to 1922. The leading lights of Welsh patriotism, to whom the Davies family were connected by family ties and friendship, had great success in that period in creating a variety of national institutions, of which the National Museum and the National Library, both founded in 1907, were only a part. However high the Victorian moral endeavour of their circle, it is striking that many of the Welsh patriots of this period, like the Davies sisters themselves, had strong aesthetic leanings.

All these elements – commerce, religion, politics, patriotism and even touches of aestheticism – were to be found in Welsh leaders of the later nineteenth century, but historians discern a gradual change in each generation. The grandfather of Gwendoline and Margaret, the famous industrialist David Davies of Llandinam (1818-1890), was an intensely pious Calvinist (who would never open a letter on a Sunday, for example) and, like all his family, an uncompromising teetotaller (at the party he threw for the coming of age of his son Edward in 1873, the toast was accompanied by the popping of twelve thousand lemonade bottles). The Davies sisters were connected closely through their mother, stepmother and grandmother with the family of John Jones of Talysarn (1797-1855), the most famous preacher of his age, a Calvinist leader and successful developer of the Dorothea slate quarry in Caernarfonshire. One of Jones of Talysarn's daughters was the mother of G. M. Ll. Davies, pacifist MP for the University of Wales and later

Right: Gregynog Hall, the Montgomeryshire country house bought by the Davies sisters in July 1920 to be used as a centre for arts and crafts and for conferences. It became their home in 1924.

warden at a workers' settlement at Maesyrhaf, and J. Glyn Davies, who created the nucleus of the National Library at the college in Aberystwyth. J. Glyn Davies had a blazing row with John Humphreys Davies (who later became Principal of Aberystwyth in the teeth of the Llandinam family's opposition – they wanted Thomas Jones), who was the descendant of the Methodist leaders David Charles (brother of Thomas Charles of Bala), Lewis Edwards (Principal of Bala College and father of Thomas Charles Edwards, inaugural Principal of Aberystwyth) and the Methodist stormy petrel Peter Williams. This family was connected by marriage to that of Thomas Charles Edward's colleague, Thomas Jones of Denbigh, the ancestor of Sir Herbert Lewis MP, a close friend of T. E. Ellis MP (brother-in-law of John Humphreys Davies) who campaigned for years for the establishment of a National Museum-cum-Library. Dora Herbert Jones, having been secretary to Sir Herbert Lewis, became a close associate of Gwendoline and Margaret's during the First World War and was their secretary for many years. Gwendoline told Dora that in her youth she had been expected to attend chapel every night of the week save one, such was their family tradition.

These kin-group connections must not be over-done, but many of the late nineteenth-century leaders came from a religious background: Sir John Williams, Queen Victoria's doctor and an obsessive bibliophile, who was instrumental in determining that Aberystwyth would be the home of the National Library, was originally intended for the ministry, as was Sir Owen M. Edwards. Sir David Brynmor Jones and Principal Viriamu Jones, strong supporters of Welsh national institutions such as the Museum and the University, were the sons of a Congregationalist minister in Swansea. Dr Thomas Jones CH (1870-1955), the greatest influence of all on Gwendoline and Margaret, left Rhymney for Aberystwyth with the intention of entering the Calvinist ministry, and it was through his close friend Richard Jones, Calvinist minister of Llandinam, that Thomas Jones was introduced to the Davies circle and thence to Lloyd George. Lloyd George, although entirely secular in his attitudes, came from the deeply dissenting background of the Campbellite Baptists. Thomas Henry Thomas 'Arlunydd Penygarn', an important figure in reorganizing the Gorsedd of Bards and a powerful spokesman for establishing the National Museum in Cardiff, was the son of the Principal of the Pontypool Baptist College, Alfred Thomas MP (later Lord Pontypridd), who was also a keen supporter of the National Museum, left a generous legacy to found an art gallery in Cardiff and was a Cardiff Baptist. James Pyke Thompson of Penarth, whose collection formed the nucleus of the art department of the new National Museum and built the Turner House Gallery in Penarth, came from a Unitarian background. Saunders Lewis, who founded Plaid Genedlaethol Cymru in 1925, was the grandson of Dr Owen Thomas of Liverpool, author of a celebrated biography of John Jones of Talysarn.

David Davies of Llandinam and his family were Welsh-speaking, but he was well-known for warning his fellow countrymen that if they wanted to progress in life they must learn English, thus reflecting many of the criticisms of Wales made by the three commissioners in their 1847 Report on Welsh Education that became known as the Blue Books. Besides his businesses and his chapel, he became intensely interested in educational progress. Sir Hugh Owen, civil servant and technocrat, is famous for having gone around Wales begging for contributions to found the University College of Wales in 1872 at Aberystwyth. David Davies's contributions were by far the largest. This was the first national institution patronized by the Davies family, who took an almost proprietorial interest in it over many decades. This also indicated a great cultural shift in the latter half of the nineteenth century, from the Protestant work ethic to a social and educational conscience and political action. David Davies became MP for Cardiganshire in 1874, campaigning in a waggonette drawn by four horses and with two postillions. Although the aim of David Davies and his associates was to produce a useful English-speaking middle class, the college was seen by its early students, such as Sir John Edward Lloyd, Sir Owen M. Edwards and T. E. Ellis MP, as a Welsh national institution and a prototype for many others. They conveyed this enthusiasm to a slightly younger generation of students, such as Thomas Jones, who was a student in Aberystwyth in 1890.

The ambiguous effects of the strictures of the Blue Books can be seen in the strong desire to learn English in Victorian Wales, but also in the sense of shame that Wales did not possess national institutions of her own. The families we have mentioned, kinsfolk and friends of the Davies family in many cases, set about developing Welsh institutions in the last third of the nineteenth century. The Davies family were members of the *Hen Gorff* ('Old Body'), the Calvinistic Methodist Connexion that had separated from Anglicanism in 1811 and formed a powerful national institution. The Baptists and the Independents formed their own nationwide unions. A national museum-cum-library was proposed at various meetings in the 1850s and 1860s. The Honourable Society of Cymmrodorion was revived in London in 1873, and provided a London platform for discussing Welsh causes. Many of the MPs elected after 1868 were more self-consciously Welsh than the previous generation, aware that in this they were reflecting their constituents' greater concerns for Welshness and Nonconformity. On a more popular level, the Welsh Football Association was founded in 1876 and the Welsh Rugby Union in 1880; artists formed The Royal Cambrian Academy in 1882, University colleges opened in Cardiff in 1882 and Bangor in 1884, The Welsh Language Society appeared in 1885, while in 1886 the *Cymru Fydd* league or 'Young Wales', with a mild programme of national devolution for Wales, was formed. In 1888 a Welsh National Musical Association was formed and the Gorsedd of Bards was set on a firm basis, and a separate system of secondary schools was set up for Wales in 1889. Liberal politicians such as T. E. Ellis, Alfred Thomas and Herbert Lewis failed in their attempts to link the new Welsh county councils in a sort of national council in 1892, and the Cymru Fydd movement petered out about 1896. However, Welsh pressure was sufficient to link the three colleges of Aberystwyth, Bangor and Cardiff together in a federal University of Wales in 1893. Educational devolution for Wales continued with the Central Welsh Board (for examinations) in 1896 and in the same year the Royal Commission on Land in Wales reported.

The Liberals, who formed the great bulk of Welsh MPs, found themselves in opposition from 1895 to 1905 and busied themselves with promoting Welsh causes such as the disestablishment and disendowment of the Anglican Church in Wales and the foundation of a state-funded national museum and library. Various Welsh agricultural bodies were formed in this period, the largest being the Royal Welsh Agricultural Society in 1904 – in which the second David Davies (Lord Davies) was to play an exceptionally important part. The Government came under great pressure from all Welsh public bodies and changed tack in 1903, leading to the various negotiations that set up two institutions in 1907 – the National Library in Aberystwyth and the National Museum in Cardiff. By this date, the Liberals were again in power, and Wales was given its own department at the Board of Education followed in 1908 by the Royal Commission on Ancient and Historic Monuments in Wales. The Welsh Council of Agriculture came in 1912 and the separate National Health Insurance Commission for Wales in 1913, leading to a Welsh Board of Health in 1919. The seemingly interminable process of disestablishing the Church became law in 1914.

That list is surely enough to show that the generation born in the middle decades of the nineteenth century, although often from a religious background, had begun to think of social improvement and secular national institutions from the 1870s onwards. This was also a period of immense economic expansion and prosperity right up to the First World War and beyond, but it was also a time of the growing secularization of the working classes, their rapid unionization in the 1890s – the South Wales Miners' Federation came in 1898 – and with it growing militancy. This, perhaps, created a sense of guilt and unease in several capitalist families over the sources of their inherited wealth. The Davies family were certainly noted for their strong social conscience. Even before the sisters had begun to collect paintings in 1908, they had made gifts to their college at Aberystwyth, the most notable being the Chemistry department, the Edward Davies Building of 1907 on the Buarth hill above the town. King Edward VII died in 1910 and David Davies the younger immediately set about founding the King Edward VII Welsh National Memorial Association to eradicate tuberculosis, the scourge of the Welsh countryside. Thomas Jones (a young professor at Belfast) was appointed its secretary, and the Davieses contributed generously to building sanatoria across Wales, a medical research centre at Cardiff and endowing a chair in tuberculosis at the Welsh School of Medicine in 1921. This set a pattern for the family's philanthropy for the rest of their lives; they maintained summer holiday camps at Boverton (not far from their port of Barry) for children, a holiday home at Llwyngwril on the coast of Merioneth for sick girls and even a kind of almshouse at Folkstone for elderly women. They also sustained the University College at Aberystwyth, for example with an Arts and Crafts Museum founded in 1918 (David Davies was college President from 1926), the National Library (he was its President from 1927) and the National Museum.

Just as Anglophile capitalism had given way to a Welsh consciousness and a social conscience, so killjoy Puritanism began to yield grudgingly to aestheticism. Graven images should never be worshipped, but were perhaps tolerable if they were ultimately destined for a national gallery. T. E. Ellis, who inspired so many of the younger generation and had himself come under the influence of Ruskin and William Morris at Oxford, wished to imbue the Welsh with a new love of beauty. Owen M. Edwards made repeated efforts to bring artistic awareness to the common folk of Wales by peppering his books and journals in Welsh with pictures. Sir John Williams was a great buyer of pictures and prints, as well as being an obsessive collector of ancient manuscripts and books. Sir Herbert Lewis had a strong artistic sense and with his wife helped to found the Welsh Folk-Song Society in 1906 – hence his secretary Dora Herbert Jones's passion for folk-song. The third marquess of Bute, far richer than the Davieses, was a lavish restorer of ancient castles such as Cardiff Castle and Castell Coch. Richard Glynn Vivian spent his part of the Vivian copper fortune on collecting pictures and on the gallery in Swansea that still bears his name. The Coombe-Tennant family, industrialists of Cadoxton, Neath, patronized Welsh artists such as Evan Walters. T. H. Thomas 'Arlunydd Penygarn' got together with the artist Hubert Herkomer and others around 1890 to conjure up the pageantry of the Gorsedd of Bards, so as to improve the visual impact of the National Eisteddfod. Peter Lord, in his book *Industrial Society*, has many other instances of the association of art with industry, and in *Imaging the Nation* he indicates how much more artistic awareness there was in Wales from 1880 onwards.

The First World War, it is generally agreed, had a profound effect on Welsh life. The optimism of Edwardian society, its religious faith and its belief in material progress had evaporated; the coal boom following the war quickly gave way to strikes, depression and the slump. The Victorian Wales of the Davies family had not been entirely parochial, for their commerce and industry had involved trade across the world and they contributed to Calvinist missions in the Himalayas. But the Great War and the economic crises had made the Welsh realize far more deeply that their fate was bound up with that of other countries. David Davies had quarrelled with Lloyd George, but he remained a Liberal MP up to 1929 at the time of the break-up of the Liberal party. He became deeply obsessed with the Versailles Settlement and international peace. In 1922 he helped to set up a Welsh branch of the League of Nations Union, and in 1936-8 paid for building the Temple of Peace in Cardiff as its headquarters. Many of the conferences held at Gregynog by the two sisters were for international peace causes dear to their brother's heart. They and their friends, such as Thomas Jones, found themselves helplessly floundering in the 1920s and 1930s, trying to find answers to the crisis that seemed to hit hardest the very areas (such as the Rhondda) from which they drew their wealth – hence the large number of meetings to solve the problems of the 'Distressed Areas', with the help of bodies such as the Welsh Council for Social Service. The National Council of Music (run by the University of Wales), which Gwendoline and Margaret had largely founded with their friend Sir Walford Davies with a crusading aim to bring music to the people, regarded Gregynog as its headquarters and did truly heroic work in creating classes, chamber groups and festivals across the industrial valleys during the dismal days of the slump. The Council's furniture removers lugged one hundred and fifty pianos from concerts to classes across the valleys during the 1930s.

In 1944, the two sisters were devastated by the loss of their brother David, followed soon afterwards by the death of his son Michael in action. Gwendoline died in 1951, Margaret in 1963. Gregynog was left to the University of Wales in 1960 as a conference centre, while the pictures went to the University College of Wales in Aberystwyth, the National Library and, above all, to the National Museum in Cardiff. These closing moves were entirely appropriate. These Welsh national institutions bore the hallmark of the Davieses and their class. Not that the two sisters sought personal fame. Thomas Jones records a conversation with Mrs Stanley Baldwin in 1932, explaining to her surprise that the two sisters were only tepid in their reaction to the news that their brother had become Lord Davies: they would prefer him to be plain David Davies. He tried to explain, to her incomprehension, their ethos of 'democracy and anonymity'. The world of the Davieses, their friends and kinsfolk in the Nonconformist elite of late Victorian and Edwardian Wales was one of high moral endeavour, philanthropy and altruism, a soulful yearning for things of beauty and the creation of national institutions for the Welsh. The world of the Davieses has gone, but we are all still taking advantage of its heritage.

Right: Pierre-Auguste Renoir, *La Parisienne*, the best known painting in the Davies collection at the Museum and a key work in the First Impressionist Exhibition in 1874. Gwendoline Davies saw it in the National Portrait Society exhibition at the Grosvenor Gallery in London and bought it in March 1913 for £5,000.

'WHATSOEVER THY HAND FINDETH TO DO'

THE 'TOP SAWYER'S' LEGACY

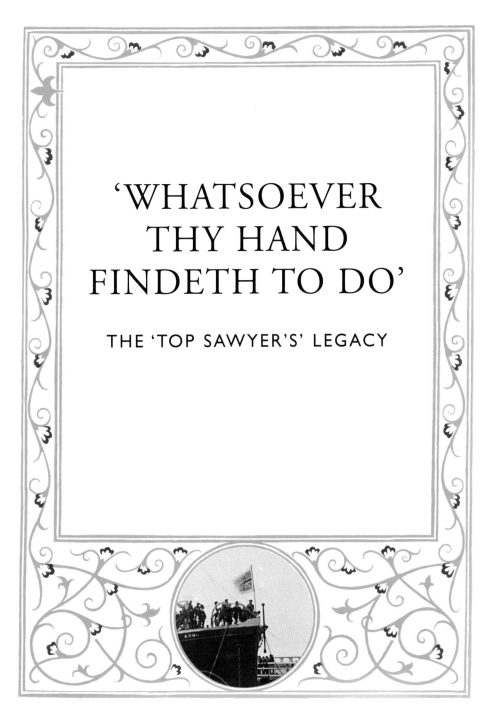

THAT GWENDOLINE AND Margaret Davies were considered among the wealthiest women in Britain in their youth was directly attributable to their remarkable grandfather, David Davies. The son of a tenant farmer, brought up on the smallholding of Draintewion near Llandinam in Montgomeryshire, he soon began to display a precocious although quite untutored talent as a quantity surveyor and civil engineer. Almost at a glance, he could tell how much useful timber could be extracted from a felled tree or how long it would take to build an embankment. He became the contractor for road bridges and a considerable part of the railway system in mid-Wales, a pioneer in the coal industry in south Wales and the driving force behind the construction of Barry dock. His fervent adherence to Calvinistic Methodism made him a lifelong Sabbatarian and teetotaller. It also instilled in him a profound sense of philanthropy and public service; he gave generously to religious and educational causes (especially the infant University College at Aberystwyth), served as MP for Cardigan Boroughs during 1874-86 and was elected to the first Montgomeryshire County Council just a year before he died.

David Davies's talents as a civil engineer came to light when he built embankments along the River Severn to protect the lands of Gwerneirin, Llandinam, where he was farming at the time. The embankments came to the attention of Thomas Penson, then county surveyor for Montgomeryshire. Penson invited Davies to undertake a number of bridge-building contracts on Montgomeryshire's road system. Another early contract was a new cattle market at Oswestry. And when the railway age encroached upon mid-Wales, Davies was swift to apply his skills to the construction of the new transport network. His first line was the Llanidloes & Newtown, opened in 1859. In the early 1860s the excavation of the great cutting at Talerddig was a crowning achievement during the construction of the Newtown & Machynlleth Railway – at the time, it was the deepest in the world. Other lines in north and west Wales followed (although his commercial good sense did desert him slightly with his involvement with the ill-fated Manchester & Milford Railway – which reached neither location).

Chapter opening: The quote 'Whatever thy hand findeth to do, do it with thy might' is from Ecclesiastes Ch. 9 v 10, and appears on David Davies's grave. The picture shows him in a rare moment of repose.

Right, top: Davies's childhood home, the smallholding of 'Draintewion' high on the hillside overlooking Llandinam. The name means 'dense brambles', giving some idea of the battle once fought with nature to create a viable agricultural holding at this location.

Right, bottom: Davies's first public contract was the construction of the approaches and abutments to this handsome iron bridge across the Severn at Llandinam in 1846.

Although Davies's achievements as a railway builder were remarkable, it was coal that would come to be at the heart of the Davies family's fortune. Taking many of his railway navvies from mid-Wales south with him, in 1864 he secured the lease of 2,000 acres of mineral tract in the Rhondda, and two years later the Maindy and Parc pits were in production. He then leased a further 8,000 acres, extending westwards to the heads of the Garw and Ogwr valleys, on which the Dare, Eastern, Western and Garw pits were sunk between 1870 and 1885. The lease of another tract near Pontypridd led to the opening of the Lady Windsor pit at Ynysybwl in 1886. New communities sprang up around these pits, with a strong Montgomeryshire element in their population and, to this day, many people living in mid-Wales still retain contact with distant relatives 'down South'.

These collieries were vested in a company, the Ocean Coal Co. Ltd, with a capital of £800,000 in 8,000 one-hundred-pound shares at its formation in 1887; just over half of these shares were held by David Davies and his son Edward. The annual production figure of the company was approaching two million tons in 1890, making it the largest producer in the south Wales

Above: A stereoscopic view of the chasm-like cutting through the watershed at Talerddig on the Newtown & Machynlleth Railway, the deepest in the world when completed in 1862. Rock yielded by the excavation provided stone for the construction of buildings and bridges down the line towards Machynlleth.

Right, top: The Lady Windsor colliery at Ynysybwl, opened in 1886 and closed in February 1988.

Right, bottom: Retired veterans of the Maindy and Eastern collieries at a reunion in August 1896. Many of these would have been former railway navvies from mid-Wales who had followed David Davies south to the coalfield in the mid-1860s.

Maindy Colliery, Ton Pentre.

coalfield, while the growing importance of foreign markets for south Wales steam coal was recognized in the fact that Ocean owned the Port Said & Suez Coal Co. Ltd (which had a contract to supply bunker coal to P&O's liners) and was also the sole supplier of Welsh coal to the chain of south American bunkering stations owned by Wilson, Sons & Co. Ltd, later absorbed into the Ocean company.

It was the importance of the export markets that led Davies to emerge in the late 1870s at the head of a number of colliery owners from the Rhondda who were disillusioned with the stranglehold held by the Taff Vale Railway and Cardiff's Bute docks on the movement of coal from their part of the coalfield; both railway and docks were congested and increasingly incapable of handling the ever-growing traffic. Davies considered a number of options at the time, including constructing a new dock at what is today Ogmore-by-Sea, but his eventual solution was to build another railway from the coalfield to a commodious new dock at Barry, then a tiny hamlet. Despite fierce opposition in Parliament, the Barry Dock & Railway Act was passed in 1884, and the new railway and dock opened five years later. Within five months of its opening, over a million tons of coal had been exported, and it retained a slight edge over coal export figures from Cardiff until the peak of the coal trade just before the First World War.

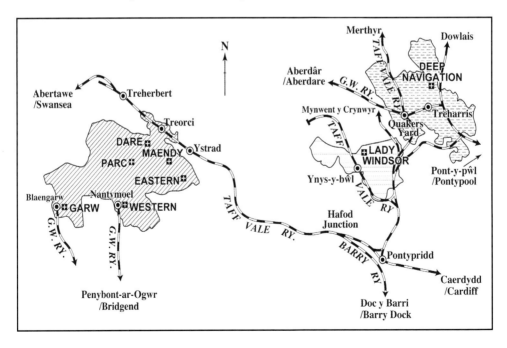

Davies's entrepreneurial skills and achievements gradually came to the attention of an international audience, and he was invited to undertake a number of lengthy foreign tours, advising on railway and civil engineering schemes. He was present at the opening of the Suez Canal in 1869, and was pleased thereafter to be able to visit Palestine and see many places of which he had read in the Bible. He also advised Tsar Alexander II on the construction of Russia's railway system. However, despite his many travels and his commitments in south Wales and London, he always considered Llandinam as home; he made every effort to be there at weekends so that he could attend chapel services, and in 1864 he built a fine new house, Broneirion, on the outskirts of the village. Twenty years later, he bought Plas Dinam as a home for his son Edward; ironically, it was formerly the home of the local gentry family, the Crewe-Reads, whose tenant Davies had once been.

The pre-eminence of the Ocean company in the years leading up to 1890 was due almost entirely to David Davies's tireless energy and drive; the company's gross profit in the unprecedented boom years of 1890-91 was a little over £470,000 – nearly £36,000,000 today. Following his death on 20 July 1890, however, the company entered a markedly less dynamic era and were

Previous spread: The Maindy colliery at Ton Pentre in the Rhondda Fawr, David Davies's pioneer pit in south Wales.

Left: The location of the Ocean collieries and the rail routes that served them in 1895.

Above: A worldwide business: Wilson, Sons & Co.'s bunkering station at Bahia in Brazil in 1906. The Wilson company was absorbed by Ocean two years later.

soon overtaken by Powell Duffryn as the foremost Welsh coal producer. A significant addition was made in 1893 with the purchase of the Deep Navigation colliery near Treharris (at 760 yards, the deepest pit in south Wales at that time); however, the idea for the purchase was originally David Davies's.

Davies's son and heir, Edward, was a gentle, scholarly man, deeply interested in chemistry and aspects of mechanical engineering. During the 1870s he pursued a lengthy and enthusiastic correspondence with the locomotive manufacturers Sharp, Stewart & Co. of Manchester regarding his design for an improved exhaust injector for railway locomotives. However, he found the responsibilities of running the massive business empire created by his father, in particular the construction of a second dock at Barry, an intolerable burden. Years later, in a letter to Thomas

Left: Edward Davies (1852–1898), Gwendoline and Margaret's father.

Above: The steamship *Arno* breaking the ribbon at the opening of Barry dock on 18 July 1898.

Jones, Gwendoline wrote '...[it was] the mental strain and stress of the collieries and Barry Docks in those early days which killed him.' He died on New Year's Day 1898, aged just forty-five; Barry's second dock, which doubled the port's capacity but had caused Edward Davies so much anguish, opened later that year.

Edward Davies's will was proved in October 1898; his estate was valued at £1,206,311 gross. The bulk of the estate was divided between his three children, though the sisters did not receive their shares of the estate outright until they reached the age of twenty-five in 1907 and 1909 respectively. Each inherited about £330,000, mostly in Ocean shares. At that time, the south Wales coalfield and its communities were booming. The industry would eventually reach its zenith in 1913, in which year the Ocean company produced nearly 2.4 million tons of coal and employed over 8,000 people. The total output of the south Wales coalfield in that year was almost 57 million tons.

The aftermath of the First World War brought about massive upheaval in Wales's economic and social structure, nowhere more so than in the coal and shipping industries of south Wales. Previously important South American markets had been lost to the USA, German coal flooded Europe as a result of the reparations insisted upon in the Treaty of Versailles, while oil was finding favour as a maritime fuel, especially in the Royal Navy, which had previously specified Welsh steam coal.

These developments unavoidably impacted on the Ocean company, especially during the depths of the Depression following the Wall Street Crash in 1929. In June 1931 Gwendoline wrote to Thomas Jones telling him how worried her brother was about the Depression: '...he can't see a chink of light'. As the dire economic situation prevailed and unemployment continued to rise, she became increasingly concerned about the unemployed miners. On 20 January 1933 she urged her brother to make sure that Thomas Evans, managing director of Ocean, allowed unemployed miners unrestricted access to the colliery tips to pick house coal. In July 1934 she was urging Thomas Jones to consider the establishment of a 'public utility company' funded joint-

Right, top: Barry No. 1 dock on the eve of the First World War, when the coal trade was at its height. What appears to be a solid level surface in the right foreground is in fact dock water, coated in a thick film of scum and coal dust.

Right, bottom: Among the sisters' more unusual investments were shares held in Bristol Channel pleasure steamers. These investments had their origins in 1905 when the Barry Railway acquired two fine new paddle steamers to operate from the passenger pier at Barry to challenge rival company P. & A. Campbell's monopoly over pleasure steamer services in the area. Here is one of those vessels, the *Gwalia*, sailing down the River Avon.

ly by the public purse and private enterprise, and in January 1935 she made a further impassioned plea to Jones, which is remarkable for its belief that a Keynesian programme of public works, comparable to Roosevelt's 'New Deal' in the USA, was the obvious answer to the economic ills of the age:

> As long as the unemployed remain quiet and patient, this
> government will do nothing – what have they done to provide wage-
> earning employment for the masses during the last five years?
> TJ, you are the man! Go to Baldwin, implore him to take the matter
> in hand immediately … call in Lloyd George, start a crusade all over
> the country! Severn Barrage, Wash Barrage, afforestation, drainage,
> waterworks, all schemes that would benefit the country in the
> long term … you would be bringing in the Socialist programme,
> but quietly, without a jar or terrible upheaval.

And this from the Top Sawyer's grand-daughter – an unsuspected radical indeed! However, at the same time, the Ocean company was attempting to weaken the influence of the South Wales Miners' Federation and promote the South Wales Miners' Industrial Union (the company or 'scab' union); in October 1935, the Parc miners staged an eight day 'stay-down' strike in protest against the employment of SWMIU members at Ocean pits.

The Depression only lifted with the onset of another global conflict in 1939, and the post-war election of a Labour government with a mandate for widespread nationalization saw the Davies family lose control over all their coal, railway and dock interests. Today, all the Ocean pits have closed, as has most of the Barry Railway system, while Barry docks see little activity. However, due to its interests in south America, a successor company called Ocean Wilsons Holdings Ltd survives to this day, registered in Bermuda and engaged principally in towage, offshore supply vessels for the oil industry and container port operations in Brazil. If the Top Sawyer would not recognize south Wales today, surely it would please him to know that a direct descendant of his original enterprise is still engaged in the extraction of energy resources and in the operation of ports, both businesses that he knew so well.

Right: The Ocean Coal Co. Ltd company demonstrated a progressive attitude towards its workforce, particularly in the provision of pithead baths. The Davies sisters (Margaret is second from left in the front row and Gwendoline in the middle) are seen here at the opening of the baths at Deep Navigation colliery – the first in south Wales – in 1916. On the extreme left in a bowler hat is Thomas Evans, managing director of the Ocean Coal Co. Ltd.

Campo Santo
Pisa.

But of all these beautiful buildings, I love the Campo Santo best, sheltered by the city wall, where in sweet seclusion sleep the ancient dead, in earth brought from the Land of Christ Himself. It is so like our peaceful English cloisters, with perfect Gothic arches, and delicate tracery, and here and there a glimpse of distant dome, or marble tower. The walls are covered with curious frescoes, from the time when men had not lost their childlike faith in things divine. One of these naïve parables of colour is the Last Judgment, by the Lorenzetti of Siena, or Orcagna, wherein the souls of men, dying, are born anew, leaving the parted lips, grown pale in death. Like little children they are borne away by angels to eternal bliss, or, snatched by hideous demons are dragged down to a hideous hell, where every loathsome vice is punished in its own fulfilment.

How curious, strange and horrible this mediæval conception of divine retribution, and how slowly it dies even in our more enlightened days! When will men truly learn that "God is a God of love, and by Him actions are weighed!"

Ancient sarcophagi, Grecian and Etruscan vases, examples of the art of ages long gone by, which inspired Andrea and Niccolò Pisano, now lie here with the dead.

'MUCH THAT IS BEAUTIFUL'

ART, TRAVEL AND LEARNING

THE ART-COLLECTING OF Gwendoline and Margaret Davies is well known. With the funds they inherited from their father Edward, they amassed a spectacular collection and became renowned as pioneer collectors of Impressionist and Post-Impressionist paintings. These were predominantly acquired between 1912 and 1923. Earlier accounts of the sisters, written from the perspective of the late 1960s, describe two retiring, unmarried women, devoted to each other, who were members of the Calvinistic Methodist Church, teetotallers and strict sabbatarians, living in isolated rural Montgomeryshire. They seemed unlikely art collectors and it was assumed that they were dependent on artistic advisers rather than having their own knowledge and taste.

Family archives detailing their education and travel have since revealed much about their lifestyles. The sisters now emerge as young women who were educated in art history, extremely well travelled in Europe and beyond and who showed at times, such as during their voluntary work in France in the First World War, both independence and determination.

As children, the sisters and their elder brother David were raised at the family home, Plas Dinam, but they later made regular use of the family's London flat at 3 Buckingham Gate, and were sent away to boarding school. There was no particular history of collecting art in the Davies family (although their grandfather and grandmother were painted by Ford Madox Brown). The sisters enjoyed riding at Plas Dinam and playing tennis, Margaret being a particularly keen player. They were also musical, and both sisters drew.

Several travel journals survive; most were written by Margaret, with only two, incomplete journals by Gwendoline. The earliest journal by Margaret is dated 1897, when she was fifteen, and details a trip to London centred around Queen Victoria's Jubilee celebrations in June of that year. This visit to London might have been the sisters' initial introduction to art. On 12 June Margaret writes 'we went to South Kensington Museum and saw the old art, china and pictures and statues'. She also records an evening viewing at the New Galleries and her admiration of sculpture at the British Museum. On 19 June she described the arrival of 'Miss Blaker' to escort her and her sister to the Royal Academy. It is Jane Blaker's brother Hugh who is often credited as being the architect of the sisters' art collection. The journal is poignant, as Margaret refers fondly to her father as 'Daddy' and describes sightseeing with him. Six months later, on New Year's Day 1898, he was dead, aged only forty-five.

Chapter opening: The chapter's title is from Margaret's travel journal of May 1909, where she describes 'grand cities, with much that is beautiful in them…'. The picture is of a page from one of Gwendoline's travel journals. *Private collection*

The girls' education was completed at a 'private residential school for ladies' called Highfield at Hendon in Middlesex. Both the sisters' school autograph books survive, revealing that Gwendoline probably attended from 1899 to 1901 while Margaret appears only to have been there from 1902 to 1903. The friendships they made during these years were enduring. Evelyn and Bertha Herring, Elsie Gemmil and Dolly Dugdale all joined them on their later travels, and Gwendoline kept up her autograph book after leaving school. Margaret is then thought to have attended the Slade School of Art as an external student. Throughout her life she was a prolific amateur painter.

The sisters began to travel widely soon after they left Highfield. They did not always travel together and certainly appear more independent of each other at this stage in their lives.

Above: Gwendoline and Margaret with their governess Jane Blaker c.1895. This shows the sisters in their early teens with their governess who was initially employed to teach them French, a language in which both were to become proficient. Jane Blaker (1869-1947) was the sister of Hugh Blaker (1873-1936) the artist, critic and collector who in 1905 became the curator of the Holburne Museum in Bath. He acted for the sisters in their early days of collecting and undoubtedly influenced the way their taste progressed. Jane Blaker remained with the family long after the girls had grown to adulthood, and became a companion to their stepmother. *Private collection*

Right: Gwendoline and Margaret on horseback at Plas Dinam c.1896-7. Both Gwendoline and Margaret enjoyed riding and are shown here outside the entrance to Plas Dinam. This was probably taken at about the time the two sisters travelled to London for the first time in 1897, just prior to the death of their father. Later in life Gwendoline wrote that 'it was only on a horse that I could feel myself and be "master of my soul" in those days and the only time one was free from the vigilant eye of dear Mother'. *Private collection*

Above: A woodcut of Plas Dinam by Margaret Davies. Gwendoline and Margaret were raised with their brother at Plas Dinam, Llandinam in Montgomeryshire. The Victorian Gothic house was built by W. E. Nesfield in 1873-4. David Davies purchased it as a home for his son Edward and his first wife Mary Jones. Margaret refers to Plas Dinam in her early London journal as 'Home Sweet Home'. On returning from their Italian tour in May 1909 she wrote 'there are grand cities, with much that is beautiful in them . . . there are lovely bits of scenery to be seen, but my home is a jolly comfy one an ... I would not exchange my hills for any others'. It was here that she and her sister initially hung their art collection. Margaret was producing wood-engravings in the 1920s and her wood blocks and tools survive. *Private collection*

Right: Photograph of the West Wing of Highfield School, Hendon. Photograph taken from *Hampton's Scholastic Directory* 1902-3. The school was founded in 1863 by Fanny and Annie Metcalfe, and became one of the largest girls' schools in the country. 'The education and culture of the individual girl is considered, rather than the requirements of high school or examination routine'. While the school was set in 37 acres of countryside, it was within easy reach of London's West End, allowing regular visits to concerts and exhibitions. The school moved away in 1914 and the house was demolished in 1931. The Davies sisters formed friendships there that were to last throughout their lives. *Courtesy of Barnet Archives and Local Studies Centre*

Little Highfield (Junior School).   *Corner of West Wing.*

➤❈ "HIGHFIELD," ❈◄

Dating from 1862.

Highfield is situated on the Main Road, between Hampstead and Hendon, in North West Middlesex.

PRINCIPAL   -   MISS METCALFE.

Private Residential School for Ladies.

Senior Department for Girls over 14, Junior Department for those under that age.

HIGHFIELD, including the Houses, School Chapel, Sanatorium, Laundry, Tennis Courts, Croquet Lawns, Cricket Field, Homestead Dairy and Cottages, extends over 37 acres of ground. Although so entirely in the country, Highfield is within very easy reach of the West End, thus affording every facility for the attendance of London Professors and Lecturers, and for the visits of girls to Concerts and Exhibitions, etc.

From the Private character of the School, the Education and culture of the individual girl is considered, rather than the requirements of high school or examination routine.

Postal Address : Highfield, Hendon, N.W.

Gwendoline was in Italy in 1902 while Margaret was still at school. In 1907 Gwendoline turned twenty-five and therefore had access to her inheritance. Margaret came into her share of the family fortune in 1909, and it is from this period that we see an increased interest in art, as well as extensive travel. Margaret attended art history lectures in Germany between November 1907 and February 1908. The lectures seem to have inspired her to collect, although her first purchase had been made the previous year – a drawing by Hercules Brabizon Brabizon, *The Algerian*.

Margaret's notes survive on what was a comprehensive art history course, covering the Renaissance through to contemporary art, given by a Miss Watson in Dresden. This introduction to art history was interspersed by gallery visits. Margaret notes that Turner was one of the 'most imaginative painters' and that he 'wonderfully painted sky and water' and that Whistler was 'a romantic impressionist who painted night as no other artist painted it'. She also studied Rodin and noted that *The Kiss* was 'the most beautiful' of his works. Later that same year Gwendoline bought Turner's *Morning after the Storm* and Margaret acquired *The Storm*, paying over £13,850 for these two works to the London dealer Colnaghi. Another undated document sheds light on the sisters' approach to art history. Written in Gwendoline's small, neat hand, it is a painstaking table of Italian artists. It covers the early thirteenth century to mid-seventeenth century and lists nearly a hundred artists working in the major cities of Italy. Together the sisters also amassed a sizeable collection of postcards, many showing paintings by the artists included in Gwendoline's table.

The sisters went to Italy to improve their knowledge of art, travelling in 1908 in a 'gay and lively motor party' and returning there in March 1909. For Gwendoline the intervening year seems to have been traumatic – 'Now I find myself once more entering the enchanted land, a twelve months older, twelve months sadder and I pray a twelve months wiser girl.' It is not clear what the tragedy was that befell her. The second Italian journey is well documented, as both their diaries survive. They travelled by train in a small party that included Mr and Mrs William Jenkins (he was managing director of the Ocean Co. Ltd), but without either

Right: JMW Turner, *Morning after the Storm*. In November 1908 Gwendoline purchased this late seascape of 1840-45 and Margaret bought its companion, *The Storm*. A letter from the dealers, Colnaghi and Co., records that 'the two Turners have been most carefully packed according to instructions' and dispatched to Plas Dinam by passenger train. Both pictures were apparently inspired by the great storm of 21 November 1840 and were among a number of works given by the artist to his housekeeper. Two years later the sisters were to purchase three more Turner oils from the same group. In January 1910 Hugh Blaker wrote to Gwendoline that 'you certainly have one of the most interesting sets of pictures in existence'. Turner's observation of the effects of light on water and atmosphere in this picture foreshadows the work of the Impressionists.

Above: Postcard of Botticelli's *Primavera*. During their 1909 visit to Florence, Gwendoline declared that the Uffizi housed 'some of the world's greatest treasures' and explained that she and her sister had a guide with whom they carefully examined each picture of the early Tuscan school. The sisters often collected postcards of the great works of art they saw but this one is the only one that she stuck into her vellum-bound illustrated journal. The did not buy works by artists of the Italian Renaissance until the 1920s when they purchased two paintings attributed to Botticelli. *Private collection*

Right: Hand-coloured woodcut of a canal scene in Venice by Margaret Davies. Margaret had visited Venice in 1908 and 1909. She enjoyed sight-seeing by gondola. She described going to Murano to see glass blowing and venturing out in the evening after dinner to see the canals by torchlight – 'it is a lovely starlit night, many like ourselves take advantage of it to wander up and down in their gondolas'. She purchased Monet's *Grand Canal, Venice* in 1912, and his *Palazzo Dario* the following year. *Private collection*

their stepmother or Jane Blaker. Gwendoline's style is altogether more descriptive and flowery, while Margaret's is more prosaic. Pisa was their first destination and by April they were there, seeing the sights and climbing the famous leaning tower.

From Pisa they travelled to Florence. Michelangelo's *David* impressed them both, with Gwendoline describing him as being 'just as strong, just as thoughtful, just as silent as when he left the master's workshop quite four hundred years ago'. Gwendoline recorded the galleries of the Uffizzi as full of paintings 'so arranged that you can trace the progress of Italian painting from its crude beginnings till it reached the zenith of its glory in the XVth century and after that the sad tale of decline'. They also visited Assisi, and saw the 'wonderful work' of Giotto in the church of St Francis, Perugia, Siena and the ancient Etruscan city of Fiesole. They then left Tuscany for Venice, stopping over at Bologna. This was a return visit, as many of the Venetian sights Margaret anticipated seeing were familiar to her. They began on 22 April and over the next few days took in the Doge's Palace, where Margaret admired *The Marriage of St Catherine* by Tintoretto, the basilica of St Mark's and the great church of Santa Maria della Salute. They left a visit to The Academia until almost the end of their stay. Margaret's description of the experience shows they took their study of art seriously: 'After watching the growth of painting in Florence, Siena and Perugia, we are going to study chiefly the School of the Venetians, the land of colour, the works of the Bellinis, of Carpaccio, the large works of Titian, of Paolo Veronese, of Tintoretto and of Palma Vecchio and many others'. They left Venice on 28 April for Paris, stopping at Milan on the way for some further sightseeing.

In Paris, the sisters visited the Louvre, which they appear to know well: 'we pass through the large halls and I pick out some of my favourites there'. Already the owners of two Corots, they were keen to see his work – 'there is a very good collection by Corot, they are indeed all lovely'. Margaret also recorded that 'There are some very beautiful tiny gems by Millet of peasant life'. In October 1909 the sisters acquired a third Corot, *Castel Gandolfo*, for £6,350. Later on that month Gwendoline purchased *The Goose Girl* by Millet for £5,355. Margaret particularly admired the 'lovely small pictures by Meisonnier' and soon had Hugh Blaker looking out for a

Right: George Romney, *Portrait of Mrs Newbery*, 1782-4. While in Paris in May 1909 Margaret records going to the Jardin des Tuileries to see an exhibition by eighteenth-century French and English portraitists of prominent women of the day. She much admired the work of Hoppner, Lawrence, Romney, Gainsborough, Raeburn, Hogarth and Reynolds. Shortly after her return she spent over £5,000 on this Romney, an expensive purchase given that she paid only £1,000 for her first Impressionist painting three years later (Monet's *Grand Canal, Venice*). The sitter was the sister of Robert Raikes, the promoter of Sunday schools. In December 1910 Gwendoline added a Raeburn of Mrs Robert Douglas, bought for £6,300, to their British eighteenth-century portraits.

suitable work by the artist. The sisters also went to the Salon for the spring exhibition at the Grand Palais. Margaret commented that 'One sees some very striking portraits, some pretty landscapes, some good groups and also many I do not care for, they are too impressionist to suit one'. She went on to admire an exhibition of female eighteenth-century portraits by French and English artists. The sisters travelled back to London on 6 May. Later on that month Margaret paid £5,355 for Romney's *Portrait of Mrs Newbery*. In August 1909 they were off again travelling for a 'happy week in Bayreuth and a pleasant time in the Austrian Tyrol' to enjoy the Wagner opera festival.

During 1910 the sisters purchased eighteen works as their enthusiasm for collecting increased. Blaker wrote that he was 'looking for a good Meissonier and Turner watercolours'. In March Margaret paid £5,250 for *Innocents and Card Sharpers* by Meissonier, the high price reflecting the popularity of the artist at the time. Two significant works by Millet purchased over the summer were the *Good Samaritan*, which Gwendoline acquired for only £997, and *Shepherdess*, which Margaret purchased for £1,105. And Gwendoline rounded off the year with two traditional but expensive purchases – she paid £6,000 for Turner's oil *Morning after the Wreck* and re-affirmed her love of British eighteenth-century portraiture by purchasing Raeburn's portrait *Mrs Douglas* for £6,300.

In autumn 1910 the sisters, Evelyn Herring and their stepmother set off on a tour of Germany, Switzerland, Austria and northern Italy, travelling in their Daimler. They had already toured by car to Italy in 1908 and knew that the Daimler would enable them to visit places off the tourist routes. Margaret's journal gives a fascinating glimpse of early car travel in Europe. They met the car in Cologne, then drove along the banks of the Rhine through Koblenz to St Goar with Margaret commenting that 'Personally I like some of the scenery one gets on the banks of the Wye or Severn much better'. They drove through the Black Forest, crossing over into Switzerland. They enjoyed walking in the mountains and by the lakesides before making for Oberammergau in Bavaria for the highlight of the tour – a chance to see the famous *Passion Play* held every ten years and traditionally much revered by the Nonconformist movement. By 22 September they had reached Riva at the northern end of Lake Garda. They drove down the eastern side of the lake, across the Italian border, towards Verona. Next day they departed early

Right: Jean Louis Ernest Meissonier, *Innocents and Card Sharpers*, 1861. Meissonier was a painter of small genre pieces, often with a military theme, inspired by Dutch seventeenth-century painters. Margaret admired his work in the Louvre in 1909. Alerted by his sister, Blaker wrote to Margaret on 17 March 1910 that he had viewed a suitable picture for her. A detailed description of the work was sent to Margaret by the French Gallery before she finally decided to buy it for £5,250. This high figure reflects the popularity of this artist at a time when Impressionist works could still be acquired for considerably less.

for Mantua where they admired the frescoes of Giulio Romano and Mantegna in the Palazzo Ducale. They made Bologna their base for a few days and enjoyed picking grapes above the city with their cousin Edward Lloyd Jones. From there they visited Rimini and San Marino and went to Ravenna to view the famous mosaics. They drove on to Padua where Mantegna's superb frescoe *The Martyrdom of St Christopher* in the Eremitani drew particular comment from Margaret – 'I must say I like Mantegna's work very much, the strength of his figures appeals to me'. From Padua they returned to Milan, and travelled back to Britain by train.

In March 1911 the sisters sailed on the P&O steamer *Morea* to Port Said in Egypt. They purchased only a few works of art during 1911. It was not until the September of that year that they acquired two works by Millet, *The Sower* and *The Peasant Family*, suggesting that they were abroad for some time. A further fragment from a journal details a visit to Greece with Bertha Herring. Margaret describes Gwendoline finishing off her sketch of the Acropolis from the balcony of their hotel room.

Another of Margaret's undated pre-war diaries survives. It records a four-month stay wintering at Costabelle in the south of France, travelling initially with Jane Blaker but without Gwendoline. Margaret took French conversation lessons, sketching lessons and learned to play golf. She appreciated the landscape of the area, especially walking on the mountain paths, admiring the cypresses and pines, the bright red roofs of the houses and the clear sea which at 'mid day is so blue against the rocks'. Perhaps her extended stay encouraged an interest in the subjects of the two Cézanne paintings her sister purchased in April 1918. Margaret also visited Nice, Menton and Monte Carlo, where she did not express the kind of austere reaction that one might expect to the gaming tables. Writing of the crowds around the casinos she commented,

Left, top: The photograph of Elizabeth Davies, the sisters' stepmother, in the International Travelling Pass issued in 1910. Margaret's September 1910 journal for their tour of Europe in the Daimler gives a fascinating insight into car travel in Europe at the time. The International Travelling Pass issued on 2 September by the Royal Automobile Club in London also survives with photographs of the car owner, Elizabeth Davies, the sisters' stepmother, who is described as 'not driving', and Archibald Harrington, their chauffeur. Elizabeth and the girls met up with Harrington and the Daimler in Cologne and Margaret's journal is peppered with her experiences of driving in mountainous conditions, on muddy roads, getting punctures, splashing pedestrians with mud and enduring day-long excursions covering 180 miles. *University of Wales, Gregynog*

Right, top: Photograph of St Peter played by Andreas Lang. The Passion Play is performed in Oberammergau only once every ten years. On arrival the sisters were joined by their cousin Edward Lloyd Jones, Jane Blaker and two of their aunts. Margaret captures the excitement of the local population making their way to see the play and mingling with the foreigners in the town. She was most impressed by the tableaux of the Last Supper and Christ's entry into Jerusalem but found the later scenes such as the Agony in the Garden and the Trial and Crucifixion a little distasteful. She left the theatre feeling 'no mortal man should attempt to act such a thing'. She had high praise for some of the actors though, writing 'I like Andreas Lang as Peter very much, what a kindly face he has, and oh how keenly one feels it when after denying his Lord he weeps bitterly'. *Private collection*

'How interesting to watch the different types that hover round, ready to pounce upon their money if they are fortunate to win something'. She was then joined by Gwendoline and their brother David, the party went to Italy and revisited the sights of Naples and Sicily.

It was in 1912 that the sisters began to collect in earnest. In January Gwendoline purchased Whistler's *St Mark's Venice, Nocturne in blue and gold* for £2,850, and acquired paintings by Millet and Daumier later in the year. By August they were clearly considering Impressionist works. Hugh Blaker wrote to them that month: 'I … am delighted that you think of getting some examples of the Impressionists of 1870. Very few English collectors, except Hugh Lane have bought them at all, although much of their best work is in America already. I expect you also know the work of Sisley, Pissarro and Renoir. These can still be got quite cheaply'. As the sisters owned a copy of Duret's *Peintres Impressionistes: Pissarro, Renoir, Morisot*, published in Paris in 1906, they were probably familiar with the art of both Renoir and Pissarro. In September 1912 they were considering works by Rodin and Monet – Gwendoline purchased a full-size cast of Rodin's *The Kiss* and *Illusions falling to Earth,* a marble carving. Then, in October, they acquired their first significant Impressionist paintings: Margaret bought *The*

Grand Canal, Venice by Monet for £1,600 (now in the Museum of Fine Arts, San Francisco) and Gwendoline bought *San Giorgio Maggiore* for £1,300 and *San Giorgio Maggiore by Twilight* for £1,000 – relatively modest sums considering what they had been paying for Turner's work. Gwendoline also purchased *Effect of Snow at Petit Montrouge* by Manet, now considered to be his first Impressionist painting, for only £240. The sisters were much taken by Monet, and the following year Margaret purchased *Palazzo Dario* and *Westminster Bridge* and Gwendoline bought three *Water Lilies* paintings. It was also in 1913 that Gwendoline made her most significant purchase to date, Renoir's *La Parisienne*, one of the key works in the First Impressionist Exhibition in 1874. She saw the painting in the National Portrait Society exhibition in London at the Grosvenor Gallery, and bought it in March 1913 for £5,000. Other purchases that year included two Carrières, two more Daumiers, a Mancini and two Rodin sculptures.

By the eve of the First World War Gwendoline and Margaret had amassed a superb collection, reflecting their interests, studies and travels. They had begun to collect Impressionist art and some of their most famous paintings, such as the Venetian Monets, were already on display at Plas Dinam. They continued to collect during the First World War, but their surviving diaries, which record life volunteering at the Red Cross canteens, shed no light on their purchases during this time. In January 1918 Margaret translated Vollard's *Life of Cézanne*, perhaps in preparation for her sister's purchase of two of the artist's landscapes. After the First World War they continued to be adventurous travellers – Gwendoline recorded a visit they made to Palestine in 1924, and in 1928 they took an escorted Thomas Cook tour to Damascus, Baghdad, Petra and the Holy Land.

Although the sisters' lives were circumscribed by their wealth and family background, they were far better educated and informed about art history than has previously been realized, and were extremely well travelled. They emerge as young women eager to learn and enthusiastic about the prospect of collecting. Their initial taste was varied, but they quickly seized the opportunities to embrace Impressionism, and by 1914 they had already assembled one of the most remarkable art collections in Britain.

Right: Paul Cézanne, *Midday, L'Estaque*, about 1879. Margaret's pre-war description of the landscape of the south of France calls to mind this picture her sister purchased in 1918, then titled the *François Zola Dam* - 'little mountain paths, so interesting to explore … tall and stately cypresses, the dark green mysterious pines, and the pale silvery olives …'. In January 1918, probably as part of the preparations for the purchase of this work and *Provençal Landscape*, Margaret translated from the French the art dealer Ambroise Vollard's anecdotal account of Cézanne's life. Later in life Margaret herself found inspiration painting in the south of France, where she eventually owned a house.

'KNOCKED TO PIECES'

THE IMPACT OF THE GREAT WAR

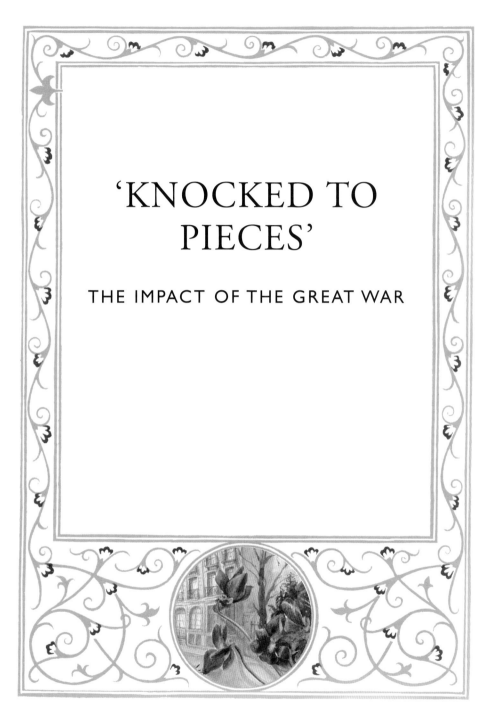

WHEN GWENDOLINE AND Margaret Davies reached the age of twenty-five, in 1907 and 1909 respectively, they each received a third of their father's estate. However, except when travelling abroad, they continued to live quietly at Plas Dinam under the wing of their formidable stepmother Mrs Elizabeth Davies. For the next few years they enjoyed a sheltered, privileged life, which was essentially private. In contrast, their elder brother David was already a busy public figure, being Liberal MP for Montgomeryshire from 1906. He also took control of his grandfather's industrial empire, seeing through the merger with Wilsons & Co. in 1908, which generated great wealth for the shareholders over the next twenty years, and assuming many other directorships. Like his grandfather, David Davies aspired to use his wealth to benefit others as well as himself, and in 1911 he launched the Welsh National Memorial Association in memory of Edward VII to combat tuberculosis in Wales. By 1929 he had given away over £250,000 in promotion of public health, higher education, housing, temperance, the Calvinistic Methodist Church and international peace. Gwendoline and Margaret remained close to their brother after he married in 1910. They also adopted a number of his good causes. They interested themselves in tuberculosis sanatoria, in the University College of Wales, Aberystwyth, and in the fledgling National Library and National Museum. The three Davies siblings jointly gave £5,000 to the National Museum's building fund in 1914. An imperious, sometimes impatient, man, David Davies associated his sisters with his own charitable work, and initially at least they were happy for him to do so. Nevertheless they also pursued a range of cultural interests, particularly in art and music, independently of him.

They started to collect art in 1908, and by 1913 they had spent over £120,000 on pictures and sculpture. Much of their collection was soon shown to the Welsh public, albeit anonymously, in a 'Loan Exhibition of Paintings' at the National Museum in February and March 1913. The idea for the exhibition came from their advisers Murray Urquhart and Hugh Blaker, and the sisters were persuaded to participate by their friend and confidant Thomas Jones. They also met all the costs of the show, which had over 26,000 visitors in seven and a half weeks. The exhibition, which included one of the most comprehensive presentations of recent French art yet seen in Britain, had a very ambitious purpose. There was a growing conviction at the time that Wales

Chapter opening: The chapter's title is from a letter Gwendoline wrote to her friend T.J. at the outset of the Second World War, where she tells him 'The first war knocked my life and health to pieces … you were the builder and the restorer.' The picture is of Margaret and Gwendoline's brother David as an officer in the Royal Welch Fusiliers, about 1915. He inherited control of the industrial empire created by their grandfather. A Liberal MP from 1906 to 1929, he served in France for a year before becoming Parliamentary Private Secretary to David Lloyd George in July 1916. Lloyd George became Prime Minister in December that year, but sacked Davies a few months later. Scarred by his war experiences, he was a passionate supporter of the League of Nations, established after the Versailles peace settlement in 1919. Created Baron Davies of Llandinam in 1932, he was a generous, if demanding, idealist who had an immense impact on Welsh life. *Private collection*

needed a revival in the arts to complement the development of national institutions and the booming growth of the Welsh economy. *The Welsh Outlook,* a monthly magazine funded by David Davies and edited by Thomas Jones, which included generous and international coverage of the arts, was clear that 'the study of painting and sculpture is in a deplorably backward condition in Wales.' The artist Christopher Williams had recently called for exhibitions of 'great pictures … to let the people know what is going on in the world of Art today.' Hugh Blaker, never one to understate his own achievements, called the exhibition 'a milestone in Welsh artistic development', and saw in its success the signs of that 'long-awaited revival.'

The idea of revitalizing the arts in Wales by the catalyst of exposure to European modernism was to resurface in the Davies family under extraordinary circumstances soon after. On 4 August 1914, Germany invaded Belgium, precipitating the First World War, which was to destroy the comfortable late-Victorian world of the sisters' childhood. The German army passed through

Above: The *Loan Exhibition of Paintings* held in the temporary museum in Cardiff City Hall, 4 February to 28 March 1913, the first exhibition organized under the auspices of the National Museum. Gwendoline and Margaret lent (anonymously) much of their newly formed collection. It included major groups of paintings by Turner, Corot, Daumier, Millet, Whistler and Monet, as well as landscape and genre paintings by other continental artists of the late nineteenth century, and two sculptures by Rodin, one of which, *The Kiss,* is prominent here.

the country, with widespread violence against civilians and private property. It was not until October, following setbacks on the Marne and the Aisne, that the Germans occupied the whole of Belgium apart from the north-west corner between Ypres and La Panne. During these weeks of chaos over a million people fled their homes. Most of them made their way to the Netherlands or to France, but around 100,000 came to Britain, where their plight attracted much interest, and a number of society ladies took on the task of finding them suitable homes. The Davies family came up with the plan that Belgian artists should be brought to Wales, where they could work in safety, and inspire the country's art students. At the end of September 1914 Major Burdon-Evans, their agent, and Thomas Jones made a perilous journey to Belgium where they assembled a group of ninety-one refugees, including the sculptor George Minne (1866-1941), and the painters Valerius de Saedeleer (1867-1941) and Gustave van de Woestyne (1881-1947) and their families. Minne's daughter Marie later described how they received 'this fantastic message from Mrs Edward Davies of Llandinam and Miss Gwen and Miss Daisy Davies; to invite Belgian artists to come to Wales, where they would not only be able to continue their work but also bring a specific talent to the Welsh people.' The sisters met the artists in London, and travelled with them to Aberystwyth. All three families were to spend the rest of the war as refugees, largely dependent on the Davies family for support. A house was found for the de Saedeleers at Rhyd-y-felin, while the Minnes and the van de Woestynes were settled at Llanidloes. Isolated from the Belgian refugee communities in London, and with no contact with other artists, the war years proved lonely and difficult ones for them. Minne, a symbolist sculptor with a European reputation without a studio or access to a foundry, could only draw. De Saedeleer struggled to support himself painting landscape panoramas of the countryside around Aberystwyth, and van de Woestyne moved permanently to London in 1916. While their impact on the arts in Wales was modest, the work of all three was to be profoundly influenced by their Welsh exile.

During 1915 the sisters became increasingly involved in charitable work in connection with the war. That summer the whole extended family was appalled when their cousin Edward Lloyd Jones, to whom Gwendoline was particularly close, was killed in the Dardenelles campaign.

Left: Portrait of Thomas Jones (1870-1955). Born in Rhymni, where his father managed the shop owned by the Rhymni Iron Company, Thomas Jones was Professor of Economics at Belfast University when David Davies appointed him secretary of his King Edward VII Welsh National Memorial Association in 1910. Jones was also the first editor of *The Welsh Outlook*, a political and cultural journal founded by David Davies in 1914. He was Deputy Secretary to the Cabinet from 1916 until 1930. Like the Davies sisters he immersed himself in many charitable and philanthropic projects. He was one of the founders of the Gregynog Press in 1921-3, and from 1930 until 1945 he was the first secretary of the Pilgrim Trust. This pastel portrait dates from around 1914 and was made in Glasgow by the Belgian artist Paul Artot (1875-1958).

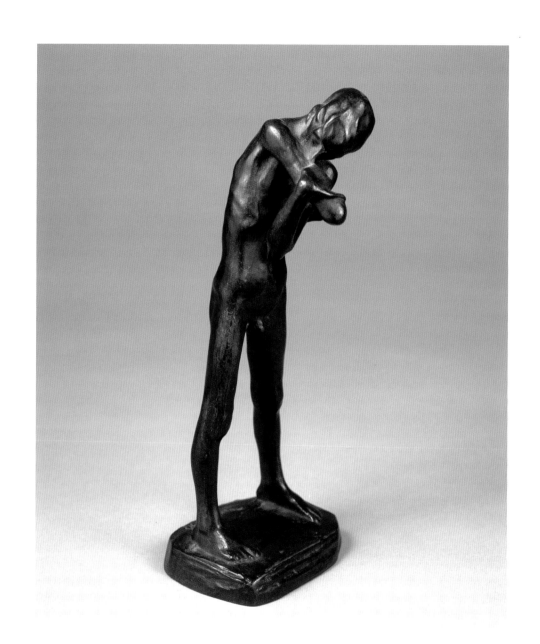

Previous page left: George Minne, *Le Petit Blessé*, 1898.
This small bronze was given to Gwendoline by the Belgian sculptor George Minne (1866-1941) in recognition of her support during the First World War. The best-known of the refugee artists who came to Wales, Minne had an international reputation as a symbolist sculptor. This sculpture shows his liking for linear elongated proportions and stylised forms, and relates to his best-known work, a fountain surrounded by kneeling youths, which was exhibited at the Vienna Secession in 1900. *University of Wales: Gregynog*

Previous page right: Augustus John, *Self-Portrait*, oil on canvas, 1913. In February 1916 Gwendoline spent £2,350 on no less than ten oils (including this one) and a drawing by Augustus John in an exhibition at the Chenil Gallery. These amounted to almost half the paintings in the show. She collected the work of no other artist on this scale, and she was determined that his work be seen at the National Museum, persuading John to donate a set of his etchings and later placing several of her own purchases on loan. © *Care of the Bridgeman Art Library/Estate of Augustus John*

Above: Valerius de Saedeleer, *Landscape near Aberystwyth / scene at Ponterwyd*, oil on canvas, 1915-21. The landscape painter Valerius de Saedeleer (1867-1941) arrived in Wales with his wife and five daughters, and was found a house at Rhyd-y-felin, near Aberystwyth. His Welsh paintings are panoramas, generally constructed on undulating decorative lines, and the almost invisible brushwork results in a thin paint surface. Works like this one, which depicts Ponterwyd, a hamlet ten miles east of Aberystwyth at the junction of the Rheidol and Llywernog rivers, proved quite popular both locally and with critics, but he had great difficulty supporting his family through painting alone. *Llyfrgell Genedlaethol Cymru - National Library of Wales*

Right: George Minne, *Mother and Child*, charcoal drawing, inscribed 'à Madame Davies / souvenir / respectueux / noel / George Minne / Llanidloes, 15'. Unable to produce sculpture during the war, Minne returned to drawing on a large scale, making hundreds that explored the theme of the mother and child, the *pieta* and the waiting woman. He even drew on the walls of his house in Llanidloes. He gave this one to the sisters' step-mother Elizabeth Davies, who was also involved in finding homes for Belgian refugee artists to Wales. *University of Wales: Gregynog*

Later in the year David Davies also went to war, serving in France with the 14th battalion, Royal Welch Fusiliers, which he had helped to raise. As it became clear that the war was going to last for several years and that victory would require unprecedented effort and sacrifice, more and more women undertook war work at home in factories, on the land, as auxiliaries or as nurses. The sisters were 'very keen to do something in the way of helping', but even in 1916, very few women managed to get out to France. One way of doing so was to volunteer, as Gwendoline did, through the London Committee of the French Red Cross. There was little provision in the French army for the welfare of the ordinary soldier or *poilu* out of the line, and the Committee sent small groups of women to operate canteens at railway stations, convalescent hospitals and transit camps, which supplied the troops with free coffee, snacks and cigarettes. These volunteers had to meet the cost of the huts from which they operated, and to find their own accommodation and living expenses. They were therefore middle-class women and some even took their maids with them. They wore Red Cross uniform, comprising a blue or white dress, a white apron with a large red cross, a headdress comprising a gauze veil and linen border, and a dark blue nurse's cape. Margaret, who joined Gwendoline in France later, was terrified of being called upon by strangers to render First Aid, and only felt comfortable in this nun-like garb when in church.

In July 1916 Gwendoline went to France as *directrice* of a small team which included her school friend Bertha Herring and Dora Herbert Jones. They were sent to the Dépôt des Isolés at Décesse, on the outskirts of Troyes, a transit camp for soldiers on their way up the line to Verdun. Their canteen, the *cantine des dames anglaises,* was a hut in the middle of the camp. Fellow helpers came and went but Gwendoline was to remain in Troyes with occasional visits back to 'Blighty' and to Paris. Margaret joined the canteen in June 1917, and her journals contain a vivid record of their life at this period. Relations with the French military authorities were not always easy. The canteen at the Dépôt was under threat of closure for months, before the *dames anglaises* were finally transferred in August 1917 to the main railway station in Troyes, where they had a reading room and a refreshment room complete with a gramophone. The *dames* had to buy food for the canteen (which was cooked by French military orderlies) and keep it clean, but their main task was to serve endless mugs of coffee or lemonade and give out a cigarette to each man. They provided writing paper and magazines, decorated the canteen with

Left: Gwendoline and Margaret's cousin, Edward Lloyd Jones, as a Captain in the Royal Welch Fusiliers. Known as 'Dolly', he was close to both sisters and travelled with them on several occasions. A thoughtful and gifted young man, he was killed in action at Suvla Bay in 1915 during the Dardenelles campaign. When his body was found, 'the watch which Daisy and Gwennie had given him' was still on his left wrist. Both sisters were deeply affected by his death and that of his younger brother Ivor who was killed later in Palestine. *Private collection*

flowers and pictures, kept the gramophone going with a mix of patriotic songs and popular music, washed the dishes, talked to the soldiers, and coped when necessary with the amorous or drunk *poilu*.

Troyes was in the *zone des armées,* and there were several British and American canteens in the vicinity, as well as a Canadian hospital. The *dames* had some leisure time and Margaret made friends among the Canadian nurses. She explored Troyes and played tennis. She also went on sketching expeditions, and the canteen workers acquired bicycles for rides in the country. Her journals are full of romantic admiration for the stoicism and courage of the *poilus,* the ordinary soldiers of the French army and of France's colonial troops from Algeria, Africa and Indo-China – she was apparently unaware of the mutinies that had brought the army close to collapse that spring. Margaret seems to have found her time in Troyes a liberating experience, as she was respected by the soldiers and her fellow workers for herself, and not for her wealth. As *directrice* Gwendoline was responsible for the management of the canteen and for its accounts, as well as for relations with the French military authorities, and with the Red Cross in Paris. For the first time she had to lead and organize others. Although travel was difficult, with long delays over permits, her trips to Paris also provided an occasional opportunity to visit the Bernheim-Jeune gallery in the boulevard de la Madeleine. She bought a Daumier and a Carrière there in April 1917, and paintings by Renoir, Manet, Monet and Puvis de Chavannes in December. In February 1918 she bought her two celebrated landscapes by Cézanne, *Midday, L'Estaque* (see page 59) and *Provençal Landscape.*

The canteen at the station had closed for repairs early in 1918, and in March, after weeks in Troyes with nothing to do, the sisters and their friends obtained permission from the Red Cross to join an American-run canteen at the station in Châlons-sur-Marne. Here they were only a few miles from the front and within sound of the guns. They were also in some physical danger as several nights saw German air-raids on the town. Margaret writes of sheltering in the canteen, listening to the rattle of the machine guns and the hum of the aeroplanes, while waiting for the bombs to fall, with only a few boards overhead as a shelter, knowing that the station must

Right: The British canteen helpers working for the London Committee of the French Red Cross were unpaid, and had to find their own accommodation. This watercolour is of the Hotel Terminus, Troyes, where both Gwendoline and Margaret stayed for a time in 1916-17. *Private collection*

Next page: The entrance to the station canteen, Troyes, where Gwendoline and Margaret worked for extended periods from August 1917. Margaret is probably the canteen worker in Red Cross uniform on the right. Next to the canteen was the *Co-operative Militaire* shop. Soon after their arrival, and to their horror, the *Co-operative* started to sell wine, but Gwendoline persuaded the Colonel in command to have this stopped. *Private collection*

Puissent
ces quelques
violettes nous
rappeler de
loin en loin
au bon
souvenir
de Mlle Derries

Julie et Marie Chéréat

Ce Janvier 1910

CANTINE des DamesAnglaises
Tout est Gratuit...

ENTREE

BOUILLON
PAIN VIANDE
16ʰ à 22ʰ

RF

SORTIE

be a target. Two French canteen workers were killed, and not being obliged to stay in Châlons, the sisters returned to Troyes at the end of the month. The war news was now very serious, with Paris being shelled by a 'mysterious big gun' and the German spring offensive making shockingly rapid progress. Weeks passed in attempts to get permission to open a new canteen elsewhere, and only mid-May were they able to re-open the station canteen. Soon after they had, for the first time, to deal with hundreds of civilian refugees from the German advance, and they were deeply moved by the suffering of the exhausted, sick and hungry women and children passing through the station. Troyes itself was full of French and American troops travelling towards the fighting, and when hospital trains evacuating the wounded stopped at the station, the canteen workers boarded them to distribute cigarettes and comforts. The sisters also visited the French and Canadian military hospitals in the town, where they tried to comfort mutilated and dying men. By mid-June the military situation had begun to improve, and a month later both sisters returned home on leave. Gwendoline was back in Troyes by the end of August 1918, but Margaret was not to return to France until after the end of the war, when she worked for three months in a canteen for British troops in Rouen, provided by the Scottish Churches.

Many British women lost male friends and relatives during the First World War, but relatively few saw for themselves the catastrophic destruction and dislocation caused by the war. Gwendoline had visited the battered, silent and empty city of Verdun in March 1917, after the end of the battle there, and in 1919 Margaret toured the British battlefields of the Somme and Ypres. They had been bombed and shelled themselves, and they had visited wounded and dying soldiers in hospital. They were deeply conscious of the horrors experienced by both British and French soldiers, and had been profoundly shocked at the suffering of civilian refugees in 1918. The stress of it all contributed to Gwendoline's increasing ill-health. Only the *camaraderie* of her fellow-workers and the sense of purpose brought her any relief. As early as December 1917, Thomas Jones noted in his diary: 'I found Miss Davies deeply affected by her life in France and determined to do all she could for the soldiers at home after the war'. Although Gwendoline continued to collect paintings after the war, this increasingly seemed an indulgence. She wrote to Thomas Jones in November 1921: 'Thank you for telling us about the John pictures – I have

Right, top: French soldiers gathered around the 'Cantine des Dames Anglaises, Dépôt des Isolés, Usine Decesse, Troyes'. Gwendoline was *directrice* of this Red Cross canteen in a transit camp near Troyes from July 1916 until August 1917, when she and her co-workers moved to another canteen in the town's main railway station. *Private collection*

Right, bottom: The men passing through the canteens in Troyes were on their way to, or from, the battlefields of Verdun and the Meuse. Many of them wrote messages in the sisters' autograph books or sent them letters of thanks. One made this sketch of marching soldiers for Gwendoline in 1918. *Private collection*

Respectueux souvenir à Miss Gwendolin Davies,
en admiration des « Dames Anglaises » qui, pour les poilus,
sont le Rayon de soleil après la triste pluie,

Léo LELÉE

Troyes, 1918=

not bought any for 18 months, we simply cannot, in the face of the appalling need everywhere, Russian children, Earl Haig's ex-soldiers, all so terribly human.' While their brother David, also permanently affected by his year at the Front, flung himself into the cause of international peace and the League of Nations, the sisters cast around for a means to repair the lives of ex-soldiers traumatized by the war, through education in the crafts and through music. Out of this grew the idea of Gregynog, as a centre for the arts and for discussion of social problems.

Left, top: The French army fought desperately for much of 1916 to prevent the Germans breaking their line outside Verdun. Gwendoline visited the damaged and largely empty city on 9 and 10 March 1917, where she acquired this postcard as a souvenir. *Private collection*

Left, bottom: Visiting the ruins of Arras Cathedral, a photograph taken by Margaret in 1919. *Private collection*

Above: After the Armistice Margaret Davies worked in a canteen in Rouen run by the Scottish Churches between March and May 1919. She may be the figure standing at the back of this photograph of British soldiers enjoying a celebratory meal. Although British soldiers sometimes passed through the station canteen in Troyes or the town's hospitals, the sisters had often hoped to be able to do more for 'our Tommies'. *Private collection*

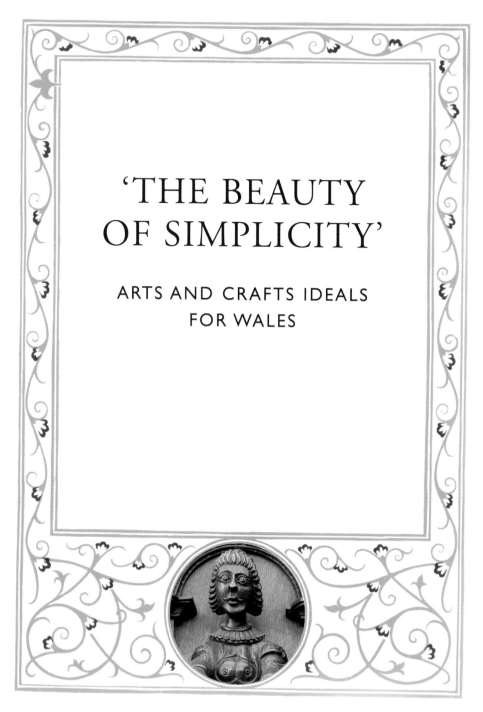

'THE BEAUTY OF SIMPLICITY'

ARTS AND CRAFTS IDEALS FOR WALES

WHILE WORKING IN the canteens in wartime France, Gwendoline and Margaret Davies were already thinking of ways in which they might support the rehabilitation of soldiers and others affected by the war. One of their ideas was to set up a rural arts and crafts community where participants could make a living out of creative work and learn new skills in peaceful surroundings. In their correspondence with Thomas Jones, they discussed the possibility of using Gregynog Hall for this purpose. The Gregynog Estate lies about four miles from Newtown, not far from the family home in Llandinam, and was familiar to Gwendoline from childhood. It had been bought in 1914 as an investment by David Davies and was let to tenants. But Gregynog was not ideal for what the sisters had in mind. It was too far away from any railway station, too large and too expensive to maintain. Gwendoline referred to Gregynog in her letters to T.J. as the 'white elephant' and suggested they 'look around for a more easily run and less pretentious place'. They relied heavily on T.J.'s advice and when they were faced with difficulties Gwendoline wrote to him 'With apologies for bothering you but you started the idea!' Realizing however that it would not be easy to find another suitable house in the neighbourhood, the sisters bought Gregynog from their brother in 1920.

The sisters hoped that creating an arts and crafts community at Gregynog would further their pre-war ambition of reviving the arts in Wales, but Gregynog was only a part of their plan to achieve this. Their longstanding concern about the state of the visual arts in Wales was underlined in a report from artist and educationalist Frederick Richards in 1918 highlighting the problems with art teaching in Wales. Two years before Gwendoline had contacted Professor H. J. Fleure at the University College of Wales, Aberystwyth, asking what would be 'the best way of making some headway with art teaching at Aberystwyth'. The Davies sisters already had close links with Aberystwyth, where their grandfather had given generously to the University College's foundation. Both Fleure and T.J. were strong advocates of the principles of the Arts and Crafts movement, which emphasized the humanizing influence of hand-craftsmanship. T.J. had studied and lectured in Glasgow where he was influenced by the work of Charles Rennie Mackintosh. He and his wife furnished their house with examples of 'honest' craftsmanship and they became, in his own words, 'furniture-conscious'. Fleure and T.J. saw the improvement of art teaching as a way to start an arts and crafts revival, but they realized that starting this in Wales, where, as Fleure wrote to T.J., 'there is so little to latch it onto', would not be an easy task.

Chapter opening: The chapter title is from a letter from Gwendoline to T.J. in April 1920, where she says 'Gregynog must be beautiful but the beauty of simplicity and usefulness'. The photograph is of some of the Brynmawr furniture the sisters commissioned especially for the bedrooms at Gregynog. *Ray Edgar*

Since the late nineteenth century, art at Aberystwyth had been taught in the Department of Education. Around 1917 the sub-department of Arts and Crafts was created with Dan Jones as the drawing master. A small number of full- and part-time students were trained in etching, bookbinding, clay modelling, weaving, furniture making and other crafts. Dan Jones was assisted by the Belgian refugee artist Valerius de Saedeleer and his daughters. Fleure and T.J. felt the art students would benefit from a teaching collection that would give 'a sketch of human workmanship in periods and regions'. They persuaded the Davies sisters to give £5,000 to build up a collection for the Arts and Crafts Museum. On T.J.'s recommendation the architect Sidney Greenslade became the Museum's 'Consulting Curator'. He was the first architect of the National Library at Aberystwyth and he designed T.J.'s house in Thanet, Kent. He is now probably better known as a friend and patron of many craftsmen of the period. A passionate collector of ceramics and glass, Greenslade was the ideal person to build the Arts and Crafts collection in Aberystwyth.

Above: Gregynog Hall has a long and complicated building history. It was rebuilt in the 1830s and around 1860-70 it was clad in concrete, making it one of the first buildings in Britain to be treated in this way. The exterior is painted to give it the appearance of a timber-frame house, typical of the area. When the Davies sisters lived at Gregynog the roof was dominated by chimneys, which were later removed. This photograph is from the 1913 Gregynog Estate Catalogue. *University of Wales, Gregynog*

Greenslade's first purchases were fine books from private presses, including the Eragny and Doves Presses and publications on the history of crafts and manuals on techniques. Archaeological material, eighteenth- and nineteenth-century glass and contemporary calligraphy were added to the collection. He purchased ethnographic objects, including musical instruments and weapons, to illustrate how different materials and techniques were used around the world. Both old and new objects were acquired so they could be compared by the students. He visited antiques shops, galleries, exhibitions and artists' studios in London and his home town Exeter to buy crafts for the Museum. The most important purchases Greenslade made were contemporary prints and ceramics. The inter-war period saw the rise of the British studio pottery movement, led by Bernard Leach, Michael Cardew, William Staite Murray, Charles Vyse and Reginald Wells. Greenslade knew many artists personally and he often bought work directly

Above: The Arts and Crafts Department at Aberystwyth around 1935 with examples of furniture and textiles made by students.

Right, top: The first prints Greenslade bought for the collection at Aberystwyth were by the architect and illustrator F. L. Griggs (1876-1938) including this etching *Priory Farm* from 1917. Griggs was associated with C. R. Ashbee's Guild of Handicraft, and this work illustrates his extraordinary technical virtuosity as well as his visionary imagination. *University of Wales, Aberystwyth*

Right, bottom: Two earthenware pots by Reginald Wells about 1922. Greenslade purchased 23 pieces of this 'Soon' ware inspired by Chinese glazes and shapes of the Song dynasty. The pots were bought with the accompanying wooden stands from the Artificers' Guild and the Beaux Arts Gallery in London. *University of Wales, Aberystwyth*

from the maker. He was particularly close to the Martin Brothers, pioneers of studio-based pottery at the end of the nineteenth century, and put together a good collection of Martin ware for the museum. Dan Jones had an interest in Welsh craft and was responsible for putting together a collection of Welsh folk crafts. He built up a fine collection of Welsh slipware to tell the story of pottery making in Wales, as well as acquiring Welsh metalwork and woodwork. Jones felt it was essential that the collection should bring 'a knowledge as well as a proper sense of appreciation of these "things of beauty"' and that it 'it would be able to instruct and inspire for the welfare of the coming generations.'

While Greenslade was developing the collection at Aberystwyth he was also helping the sisters turn Gregynog into the rural arts centre they envisaged. The former billiard room was enlarged and converted into the music room and various alterations were made to make the house suitable for its new function. Gwendoline and Margaret needed someone to organize the teaching of various crafts they hoped to establish at Gregynog. Robert Maynard was recommended by Hugh Blaker. Maynard, who had trained as an architect, spent eighteen months at the Central School of Arts and Crafts in London learning various crafts, but he was mostly interested in wood-engraving and printing and when he returned to Gregynog it was as the first Controller of the Gregynog Press. Some pottery seems to have been made at Gregynog but it was unsuccessful. Furniture making was another of the proposed crafts. Peter Waals, a furniture maker who had worked for Ernest Gimson, came to Gregynog to investigate the possibility of setting up a workshop. He reported that the work he saw in the area was below the standard of the Cotswold villages and that tradition, 'the faithful guide to the handicrafts', was entirely lost. Although Gregynog did not become the wide-ranging arts centre the sisters initially had in mind, it was to serve as a conference centre for their many philanthropic projects and a home for the Gregynog Press as well as for musical events, summer schools and weekend house parties.

The sisters had not intended to live at Gregynog when they bought the house in 1920. Their home remained Plas Dinam where they lived with their stepmother, but in 1924, after David Davies remarried, they felt obliged to leave. They moved with their art collection and some furniture to Gregynog. Gwendoline and Margaret were very private individuals and refer in letters to T.J. how difficult the loss of privacy was when the house was full of people. This might

Right, top: The Gregynog Estate catalogue from 1913 gives an idea of the furnishing of the house before the sisters bought it. They extended the former billiard room seen here and converted it into the music room. *University of Wales, Gregynog*

Right, bottom: The music room was not only used for musical events but also for conferences. It was mainly furnished with functional and hygienic cane chairs produced by the Dryad Cane Furniture Company. *University of Wales, Gregynog*

explain why almost no contemporary photography of the interiors of Gregynog exists and it is hard to establish precisely what it must have looked like. The sisters wanted the house to be simply decorated so visitors did not feel too intimidated by it. As Gwendoline wrote to T.J., using typical Arts and Crafts terminology 'Gregynog must be beautiful but the beauty of simplicity and usefulness' and 'It would be a fatal mistake to furnish it like a hydro or a luxurious private house. This would only have the effect of making them dissatisfied with their own surroundings at home.' Gwendoline and Margaret went to Heal's in London 'just to get a vague idea of the prices of things now' and did not find it encouraging. Despite Peter Waals' negative report they did commission him in the early 1920s to make some furniture for the bedrooms and library. They also bought Brynmawr furniture for the bedrooms. Furniture making was part of the Brynmawr Experiment, an attempt to relieve mass unemployment in the south Wales mining community through creating rural industries. The sisters were already involved at Brynmawr, having provided most of its funding, so ordering furniture for Gregynog fitted their ideal of supporting local craftsmanship. Chairs made by Dryad Cane Furniture of Leicester were used in the music room and bedrooms. The Waals, Brynmawr and Dryad furniture is sober, practical and made with honest craftsmanship, meeting the sisters' requirements for the simplicity in furnishing of Gregynog. As well as with these contemporary pieces, the house was also furnished with antique furniture from Plas Dinam and the sisters' flat in London. They had a taste for rather plain but elegant mahogany furniture. Gregynog housed their collection of Chinese and Islamic ceramics and other antiquities, some of which were given to the National Museum after Gwendoline's death. Contemporary ceramics included Poole and Ewenny pottery and a remarkable pelican-form jug by Charles Vyse. They also owned silver by Danish designer Georg Jensen. There were Persian carpets on the ground floor and modernist rugs in the bedrooms. To the many visitors the eclectic interiors of Gregynog must have looked an interesting mix of old and new.

While Gregynog was not initially intended as a home, Gwendoline did look forward to having her own garden 'to plan and work in'. The sisters did not make any major alterations to the existing 750 acres of gardens and woodland. Large-scale landscaping had been done in 1774 when proposals by William Emes were partly carried out, including the sunken lawns at the front of the house. The beautiful crenellated hedge of golden yew dates from around 1900. The sisters hired, unusually, a woman head gardener, Miss Clark. Gwendoline was very interested in gardening, visiting horticultural shows and buying gardening books. One of her projects was

Right: It was most likely Sidney Greenslade who designed two similar modern bathrooms for Gwendoline and Margaret around 1924, when the sisters moved to Gregynog.

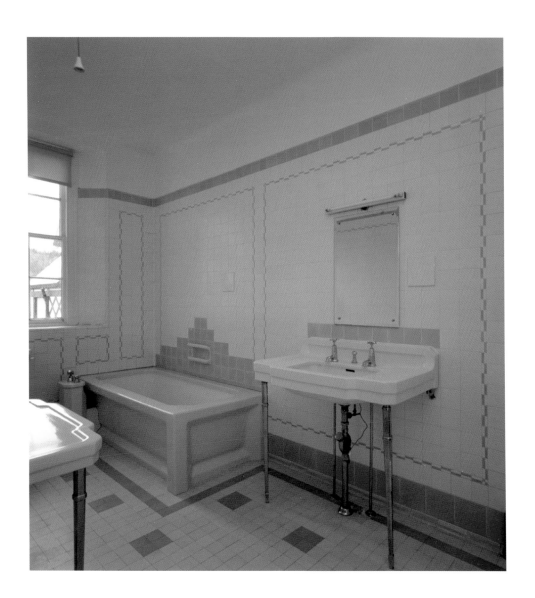

planning the lily pond, perhaps inspired by the three water lily paintings by Monet she had bought in 1913. The Arts and Crafts landscape architect H. Avray Tipping, who was a friend and adviser of Gwendoline, collaborated on the garden in 1930 with George C. Austin, who succeeded Miss Clark as head gardener. Together they created the dingle and dell. The garden also included a kitchen garden and greenhouses providing vegetables, fruit and flowers for the house. It was at its peak in the late 1930s when up to twenty-five garden staff were employed, sometimes supplemented by unemployed people from Newtown.

With work continuing at Gregynog, the promotion of arts and crafts at the University College of Wales, Aberystwyth faltered. T.J. expressed the sisters' view in a letter in 1935: 'this whole art business has been dogged by mistakes and second-raters'. To their great disappointment T.J. had not been made Principal in 1919, and a disillusioned Fleure left a few years later. In July 1933 the Department of Arts and Crafts became independent of the Department of Education, with Dan Jones as its head, but he died suddenly the next year and no successor was appointed.

The Second World War put an end to much of the work of Gregynog. By the mid-1930s it was clear that the plan of fostering an arts and crafts revival in Wales through the complementary schemes at Gregynog and Aberystwyth had enjoyed only partial success. After a visit to Dartington Hall, Devon, founded with similar ambitions as Gregynog, Gwendoline wrote to T.J. in 1936: 'It made me think of the old days when we used to dream about Gregynog, but after all it has achieved some things and the spirit of the place brings comfort and peace to many weary souls'. It had been T.J. who was instrumental in both setting up Gregynog and initiating the Arts and Crafts Museum in Aberystwyth. In spite of the sense of some disappointment over what the latter achieved, Gregynog did provide employment for people in the area and created a lasting legacy in the Press, its musical activities, the various conferences it hosted and the many visitors it welcomed.

Left: The fashionable and functional chairs by the Dryad Cane Furniture Company were used in the music room and the bedrooms. The firm was founded by Harry H. Peach, who was very actively involved in various projects to support craft education and design in Britain.

Next page, left: Furniture at Brynmawr was made under the guidance of designer Paul Matt. He designed simple furniture that could be constructed easily by a largely unskilled local workforce. In the 1930s the sisters bought many pieces of Brynmawr furniture to furnish the bedrooms at Gregynog.

Next page, right: For the library Peter Waals produced eighteen single chairs and two armchairs in walnut with rush seating and an oak table. He used materials of high quality and made a feature of constructional details, like the dovetail joints, to show honest workmanship.

Pages 94 and 95: Details from Gregynog Hall and estate. *Ray Edgar*

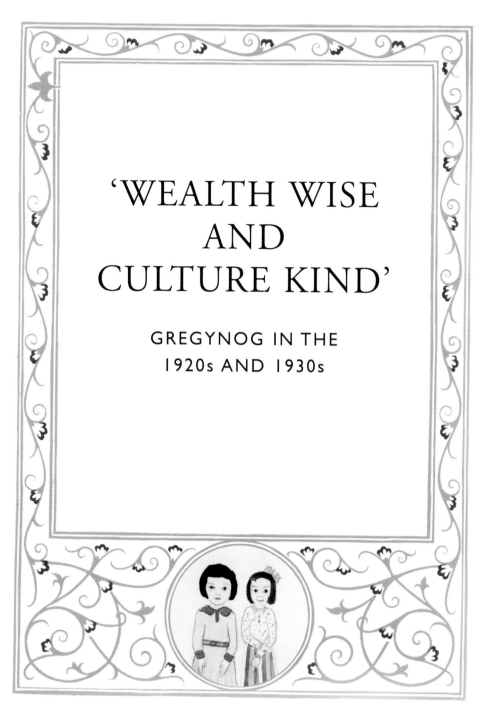

'WEALTH WISE AND CULTURE KIND'

GREGYNOG IN THE 1920s AND 1930s

A T GREGYNOG HALL, the Misses Davies commanded a large and 'well oiled' enterprise. Their imposing nineteenth-century mock half-timbered pile in rural mid-Wales could simply have been their home, a quiet retreat to receive company, but rather they wished it to be a facility they could share with many and for the benefit of others. The Gregynog Hall visitors book records a near-continuous stream of house-guests; at times up to forty might stay at the Hall, while others lodged nearby. Its renowned music festivals and national and international conferences attracted eminent visitors from near and far. One guest, Ernest Rhys, remarked of the sisters in a letter to Thomas Jones – T.J. – how unusual it was to find such 'wealth wise and culture kind'. Like T.J., the sisters were passionate champions of social, economic, political, educational and cultural initiatives in Wales. Conferences at Gregynog were among a great many causes they supported, each of which would, they hoped, go some way to build a new Wales in the aftermath of the Great War.

The League of Nations Union, National Council of Music, Welsh School of Social Service, Montgomery County Nursing Association, Welsh Schoolboys' Camp Movement, United Missionary Council for Wales and the Rural Community Councils in Wales of Educational Settlements met regularly at Gregynog during the 1920s and 30s, attended by eminent national and international educationalists, politicians and peace and social welfare campaigners. The Music Room at Gregynog, its walls lined with Impressionist and Old Master paintings, became a centre for performance, conference, argument and debate. In September 1930, for example, the Burge Memorial Trust International Conference discussed the viability of a United States of Europe: Dr Freiherr W. von Grunau, youngest son of Prince Lowenstein-Wertheim, and Dr Albrecht Mendelssohn-Bartholdy, Professor of International Law and grandson of the composer, were delegates. The Welsh National Council for Social Service in Wales met in February 1934 to discuss relief for the unemployed in the depressed areas of south Wales. Sir Crawford Eady spoke on the Unemployment Bill and William Waldorf Astor attended. Politician, social reformer and campaigner for women's rights Violet Markham participated in both the 1934 Distressed Areas of South Wales Conference on Social Work and the Fourth Annual Conference of Social Workers. In December 1937, Sir John Reith, then BBC Director General, was a speaker at the BBC Conference on Wales and Broadcasting.

Chapter opening: The chapter title is from a letter a visitor to Gregynog, Ernest Rhys, wrote to T.J. The photograph shows (clockwise from back left):Lascelles Abercrombie, George Bernard Shaw, Dora Herbert Jones, Thomas Jones, Gwendoline Davies, Margaret Davies, Jenny 'Jane' Blaker and Irene Jones. A locked mailbag was sent daily from the Hall to the post office at Tregynon where the local police took a keen interest in the great and the good visiting Gregynog. *Private collection*

GREGYNOG FIRE BRIGADE

The Welsh National Council of the League of Nations Union, one of the more influential peace organizations, met annually at Gregynog. Broadcaster, writer and regional Controller for the BBC in Wales, Alun Oldfield Davies, who attended throughout the 1930s, called it 'a talking shop' and a 'fairly high-powered conference for those days.' Delegates and houseguests were obliged to attend the Sunday services for which Gwendoline and Dora Herbert Jones had deliberated for weeks over suitable readings, prayers and music. These were well intentioned but for some guests rather solemn and disconcerting occasions. The sisters 'would have been deeply shocked,' remarked Oldfield Davies, 'at the dramatic contrast, between the Sunday morning service ... and what happened in the Upper Room, this smoke-laden room of men drinking lemonade. You'd have some of the filthiest stories told that I'd ever heard in my life.' As a 'relief

Above: Gregynog Fire Brigade (1920s). A fully trained and practiced Fire Brigade was drawn from estate workers. Gregynog was a near self-sufficient estate maintained by a staff greater in number than many a nobleman at that time could afford to retain. The head gardener and his team delivered fresh produce daily from the kitchen garden and glasshouses; a cook, butler, housekeeper, kitchen- and housemaids provided for the sisters and guests. Two chauffeurs and three limousines were on hand, and an estate manager, night watchmen, pest controller and boiler man were among the many additional staff that made sure that Gregynog ran smoothly. *Private collection*

from the rather prim, strict, religious, good feeling that existed in the house and the good manners that persisted,' the 'leaders of Welsh life, deacons, respectable people unburden[ed] themselves of a weight of guilt, dredging into their innermost subconscious and dragging up perhaps something of the spirit of the trenches, at a conference that was devoted to good will and peace among men.'

Assiduous preparation and planning were required for each event. Despite recurring ill health, Gwendoline shouldered the greater burden of responsibility. It was due to her initiative and commitment that schemes reached fruition. The sisters enjoyed company but, in a 1934 letter to T.J., Gwendoline was exasperated that Margaret had no 'conception of the nervous energy, the electric current that has to run through things to make Gregynog *alive*. "Oh! but you enjoy it" is all I get. Daisy is a brick and does splendid work but a brick is inclined to be and must be unbending and rigid.' Margaret was more at ease with guests, sociable and worldly, while Gwendoline was more circumscribed, with high expectations of delegates that on occasion were not wholly fulfilled. In a 1925 letter to T.J. she lamented that 'All sat around the fire and smoked and talked and talked and talked and smoked until midnight each night – delightful people with plenty of ideas and goodwill, but vague, nebulous and undefined.' 'I don't know what I expected a Director of Education to be like,' she wrote in 1931, 'but it all sounded so promising – the leaders ... those who are laying the foundations of time to come. They came – and we have never had such a crowd of unimaginative, hide-bound, self-sufficient, parochial minded toughs inside this house before.'

Gwendoline and Margaret were only truly at ease with guests drawn from their small circle of friends and close relations. Gwen's school friend Gina Barbour, and Margaret's classmate Bertha Herring (who accompanied the sisters on their Middle East tour of 1928), visited regularly between 1925 and 1961. In 1931 they accompanied the sisters and Violet Markham on a Mediterranean cruise, on which Charlotte and George Bernard Shaw were passengers. The following April, Markham enjoyed a weekend at Gregynog. 'One doesn't realise the full stature of the woman', Markham wrote of Gwendoline, 'till one has seen her in her own house ... To own such fantastic wealth and be so utterly and completely uncorrupted by it is a marvellous proof of the quality of her character. When one thinks of all that she has done and created in that

Right: T.J. and George Bernard Shaw at Gregynog. Shaw and his wife Charlotte were among many for whom T.J. arranged invitations to Gregynog. Shaw visited in 1930, 1932 and in 1933 when T.J. wrote how Shaw was entertaining them with talk of 'the theatre, reminiscences of Irving, Tree, and Terry and adventures of his own plays and their production.' Each evening after dinner Shaw read to the assembled company his play *On the Rocks*. Gwen told a guest: 'Charlotte and G. B. S. came over from Malvern. We enjoyed them immensely. We just let him talk—and we talked to her!' *Private collection*

place, and yet to remain so modest, so gentle, so unassuming – well, it only shows what pure gold she is made of. Riches destroy nineteen people out of twenty, more often than not they are a curse to those who own them. Gwen Davies has the true humility of soul to give them their right value and to use them without one thought of personal vanity and pomposity in the service of others. She is a great woman, and I am proud to feel she is my friend.'

Above: Lascelles Abercrombie, George Bernard Shaw and Thomas Jones at Gregynog. The poet Lascelles Abercrombie, in turn Professor of English at the Universities of Leeds, London and Oxford, was a regular contributor to the Festivals of Music and Poetry. When he died in 1938, Gregynog Press published his *Lyrics and Unfinished Poems* (1940). *Private collection*

No name in the Visitors Book appears more than that of T.J. Meeting with Gandhi and dining with Hitler, he was one of the most influential men in Europe. There could hardly have been anyone better connected than him to be their intermediary, introducing fascinating guests to Gregynog. Actress and writer Joyce Grenfell, who attended music festivals at Gregynog in the 1930s, called him a 'sort of people's impresario in the interests of others and of Wales.' As a regular guest of the Astors at Cliveden, T.J. came to know a significant number of prominent national and international figures from politics and the arts. Nobel prize-winning playwright George Bernard Shaw was among several literati connected with Cliveden for whom T.J. arranged invitations to Gregynog. Grenfell was Nancy Astor's niece, and she accompanied T.J. to Gregynog as houseguest at the Festivals of 1937 and 1938, and again on 6 April 1939 for the BBC live radio broadcast of Part 2 of Bach's *St Matthew Passion*. For her, 'staying at Gregynog was a mixed blessing. The music was unalloyed pleasure but the atmosphere in the house was cool, correct and daunting. Even T.J. was subdued by it and we sometimes escaped to go and see his old friend Dora Herbert Jones ... where it was possible to forget one's ps and qs for a while.'

Whereas T.J. introduced the literary and political guests to Gregynog, Henry Walford Davies was instrumental in bringing Vaughan Williams, Gustav Holst and Adrian Boult to the annual Festivals of Music and Poetry. 'Walford *was* the Music of this place,' commented Dora Herbert Jones, 'and everything that came, came in his style.' Walford Davies and his wife visited the Hall several times a year between July 1921 and December 1940. Sir Edward Elgar was a guest in June 1924, Ralph Vaughan Williams gave a concert in April 1932, and his friend Gustav Holst visited in July 1931 for a meeting of the National Council of Music and two years later for the first Festival of Music and Poetry. Sir Henry Wood, musician, conductor and founder of the BBC Promenade Concerts was a guest in May 1938. Poet and literary critic Lascelles

Next pages:

Joyce Grenfell (centre) and guests at Gregynog enjoy a game of tennis. *Private collection*

Bass-baritone Keith Falkner. *Private collection*

Group Photograph: The sisters enjoyed having company but Gwendoline felt she shouldered too much of the responsibility of planning. She was at times disappointed that Margaret had no 'conception of the nervous energy, the electric current that has to run through things to make Gregynog alive.' Jane Blaker (far left), Walford Davies (centre, rear), Mike Davies (front, seated left), Sir Charles Webster (kneeling behind Mike Davies), Lascelles Abercrombie (far right), Eldrydd Dugdale (soon to be Mrs Mike Davies, kneeling, right). *Private collection*

Stanley Baldwin plants a copper beech by the lake at Gregynog (1936). For the sake of his health, Prime Minister Stanley Baldwin stayed at Gregynog during August 1936. 'What a country! What peace! And what healing air!' he wrote to T.J., 'I am soaking in the Welsh spirit and if I don't make a lovely speech about 'em one day, I'll eat my hat.' *Private collection*

Abercrombie came as a regular contributor to the Festivals. Soprano Dame Isobel Baillie and renowned contralto Mary Jarred were regulars, whilst soprano Elsie Suddaby stayed twenty-six times between 1925 and 1961. Keith Falkner, the baritone and soloist, visited seven times between May 1931 and the last Festival in July 1938.

Surprisingly, not nearly as many artists or craftsmen were houseguests at Gregynog and none, save perhaps Murray Urqhuart, developed friendships with Gwendoline or Margaret. The Press naturally brought artists to Gregynog; Hughes-Stanton, Hermes, McCance and Miller Parker all stayed in May 1930, and Paul Nash, who designed the binding for *Shaw Gives Himself Away*, visited in March 1939. A watercolour of the garden that he painted from his bedroom window was purchased by Margaret in March 1957 (see page 156). Sir Matthew Smith RA visited in April 1957; three years later she had acquired three of his important canvasses.

Hugh Blaker's name is now synonymous with the Davies collection, but by the time the sisters moved to Gregynog they were no longer actively collecting. Throughout August 1923, he and Urquhart led a Summer School of Arts and Crafts; students painted in the grounds by day and Blaker led discussions on the art collection in the evenings. One of their gifted young students was Ceri Richards, who remained appreciative of this his first encounter with modern French art. Blaker signed the Visitors Book on just two other occasions, reinforcing perhaps that theirs was a professional relationship. There is also little to suggest that they received visitors express-ly to view their art collection. Winifred Coombe Tennant of Cadoxton, near Neath – collector, patron and promoter of art in Wales and Welsh artists beyond Wales – stayed four nights in March 1926, and Charles Aitken, Director of the National Gallery at Millbank, visited in October that year. Caroline Lucas and her sister Frances Byng-Stamper, patrons and founders of the Millers Press in Lewes, Sussex, were houseguests during the National Eisteddfod at Machynlleth in August 1937. That year, together with the Davies sisters, they were founder members of the Contemporary Art Society for Wales.

Gregynog's reputation as centre of the arts was immense; May Morris of Kelmscott Manor vis-ited the sisters on 11 August 1937. Consultants came periodically. Architect Sidney Greenslade visited with T.J. on four occasions between 1922 and 1932, advising the sisters on the conver-

Right: Photograph of Gwendoline Davies by Vandyck (1937). T.J. arranged that Gwendoline be made Companion of Honour. After the Investiture on 10 June 1937 he gave a luncheon party for her at the Athenaeum to which he invited Walford Davies. T.J. wrote: 'I gave one toast "Our Youngest Companion", and Gwen smiled and blushed and never looked sweeter. I packed her off presently in a taxi, against her will, with Walford, to Vandyck's to be photographed.'

sion of Gregynog. Paul Matt, manager of the Brynmawr Furniture Company, visited in 1931, 1933 and 1936, and garden designer, author and *Country Life* contributor Henry Avray Tipping visited during 1928 and 1930.

For Prime Minister Stanley Baldwin and his family, Gregynog became a refuge in August 1936; the abdication crisis had played heavily on Baldwin's health and he was persuaded to take a three-month holiday to be well in time for the Coronation. T.J. arranged that the first month should be spent at Gregynog. He and the sisters welcomed the Baldwins then departed for Broneirion, leaving their guests to Dora Herbert Jones. Persuaded that it was in the interest of the Prime Minister's health, a hamper of spirits had been ordered from Harrods on sale or return. Baldwin wrote to T.J. of 'the wonderful Dora next door, anticipating my every wish. What a country! What peace! And what healing air! I am soaking in the Welsh spirit ... I think Mr Anderson [the butler] likes pouring out wine: he hugs his bottles and plies me with assiduity. I had great difficulty in getting water out of him ... What a parasite I am! But I like it!' In appreciation, he planted a copper beech by the lake in a ceremony that was attended by Mrs Edward Davies.

Yet Gregynog and the sisters' hospitality were not to be the sole preserve of the great and the good. Their interest and concern for the welfare of others would include tenants and residents of surrounding parishes. There are innumerable records of individual acts of kindness, charitable fêtes for local causes and Christmas parties when every child in the village was presented with a book according to their ability. Children were especially welcomed at Gregynog. Staff and young girls visited from the Ty Gwyn Convalescent Home at Llwyngwril, another of the sisters' projects, and the Boverton Girls' Camp, of which Margaret was Patron. T.J.'s daughter Eirene took a group of Commonwealth children there in 1931; at a farewell party, Margaret participated in fancy dress while Gwendoline looked on. Mary Hackett stayed at Gregynog in 1938 through the Lady Frances Rhyder Overseas Student Scheme. In a letter home to her parents in

Right, top: A visit by Dutch Schoolchildren. After the War, large parties of Dutch children were brought to Wales taking over the Hall for long holidays. Thirty-seven children came between 21 June and 24 August 1945, twenty-six between 2 October and 29 November 1945, twenty-seven during 28 February–24 April 1946, and twenty-two in the summer of 1946. Local children were invited to play with visiting Dutch refugees. To the left, Jane Blaker is seated with her Old English Sheepdog, Nelson. Gwendoline, wearing a jacket and necktie, sits in the centre with Margaret, right. The black spaniel, far right, belonged to the housekeeper, Mrs Ingram. *Private collection*

Right, bottom: *Look! The first week. Look! The eighth week.* At the end of their visit, several of the Dutch children painted small watercolours in the Gregynog visitors book. Margaret Heymans expressed her gratitude to the sisters with drawings that illustrate her transformation into a healthy, rosy-cheeked girl who has been sent on her way with a stuffed WVS sack over her shoulder. *Llyfrgell Genedlaethol Cymru – The National Library of Wales*

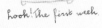

Look! the first week.

Look! the eighth week.

Margriet Heymans

Queensland, Australia, Mary described arriving by chauffered car and her impressions of the house, its paintings and sculptures, gardens, lake and the woods. She was introduced to Sir Walford and Lady Davies and after dinner they all did a crossword puzzle, the prize being a recital by Walford. 'Such dears,' she wrote, 'and so easy to converse with.' Mary accompanied the Misses Davies to chapel, called on Dora Herbert Jones for tea where 'tongues wagged hard all afternoon' and painted alongside Margaret who, dressed in smock and large-brimmed hat, painted in the meadows or the dell. Gwendoline took her in the Daimler for a day out in the countryside where they picnicked at the roadside. One evening they threw a party for Guides camping nearby, and sang around the campfire.

Gregynog was a haven too for the nephew of the cook and housekeeper, Fanny Evans, later a companion to Margaret in old age. Orphaned aged ten, John Christopher stayed for long periods from 1937 to 1948. His recollections of summers at Gregynog provide a fascinating insight into the lives of the sisters and their privileged existence on a largely self-sufficient estate – replete with fire brigade – and a staff greater in number than many a landed nobleman could afford to retain between the wars. Numerous gardeners ensured fresh produce was delivered daily from the kitchen garden and glasshouses for the sisters, their staff, delegates and houseguests.

With the coming of the Second World War, the sisters remained at Gregynog, but the Festivals and conferences ceased, the Press wound down, and the Hall was turned over to the Red Cross as a convalescent home for servicemen and civil defence workers from the Midlands. T.J. continued to send occasional guests. In November 1940, he wrote to Gwendoline from Paddington with news of the relentless bombing and widespread destruction across the city. He asked if she might accommodate the A.R.P. warden in the Adelphi and his family for a short holiday: 'Mrs H. is nearly as done up as her husband ... This would be a real kindness ... I'll go halves with you in the railway fares.' Sir Lewis Casson, Director of Council for the Encouragement of Music and the Arts, and his actress wife Dame Sybil Thorndike were guests in January 1942 after visiting the Maes-yr-Haf Settlement, and Lord and Lady Macmillan came from Sussex for two weeks in 1944 to escape from beneath the flight path of returning bombers. Between the summer of 1946 and 1947, four parties of Dutch children, who had been affected by the War, were brought to Wales for a holiday; on average there were twenty-eight in a group and each visit lasted two months.

Right, top: Gregynog House Party, Michael 'Mike' Davies at the wheel. The sisters' nephew Mike Davies could have been successor of the 'Gregynog tradition' but he had been killed in action at Rousel, Holland in 1944. *Private collection*

When Gwendoline died in 1951 there was no obvious successor to pass on the mantle of the 'Gregynog tradition'; nephew 'Mike' Davies, of whom they were especially fond, had been killed in action in 1944. T.J. died in 1955. While spending more time in the south of France for the sake of her own health, Margaret kept up such activities at Gregynog as she was able to host during her final years. There were music concerts organized by Ian Parrott, Gregynog Professor of Music at Aberystwyth, and in 1956 Lambert Gapper of the Art Department brought Sir Herbert Read to speak at a residential conference. A number of meetings discussed possible future uses for the Hall but, without Gwendoline, its 'chief creator and inspirer', and T.J., its guiding force, Gregynog's heyday was never to be revived. In a letter to T.J. written at the out-set of the Second World War, Gwen expressed her gratitude to her mentor:

> 'The first war knocked my life and health to pieces. It had to be
> rebuilt and you were the builder and the restorer. I want to thank
> you from the bottom of my heart for all you have given me and
> done for me. All I have been able to do during the last thirty years
> has been almost entirely your doing.'

Gustav Holst   July 1933

'FLINGING SONGS ACROSS THE ETHER'

THE SISTERS, GREGYNOG AND MUSIC FOR WALES

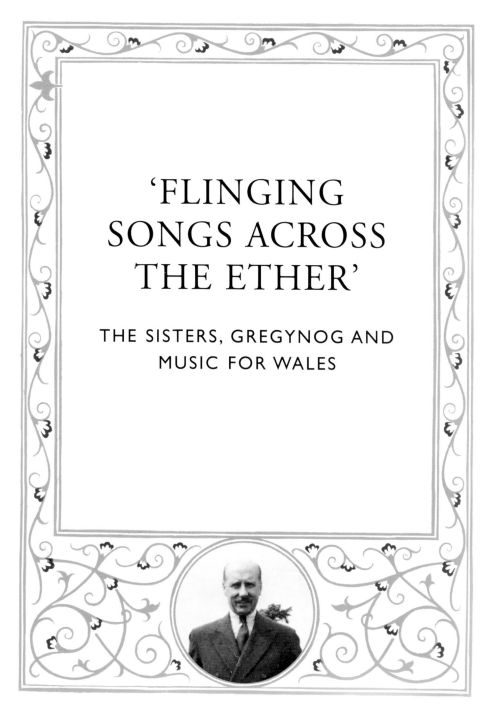

WRITING IN *THE Liverpool Daily Post* in 1936, A. K. Holland described the fourth Gregynog Festival of Music and Poetry as 'Art for love's sake'. This description, which also notes the 'intimacy, charm of atmosphere and sense of community with which the distinguished artists take part in and manage to infuse their labour of love', to an extent reflects the attitude of Gwendoline and Margaret Davies towards music in more general terms, and goes some way to explain why their practical and financial aid helped to transform the musical life of Wales in the twentieth century.

In order to understand the importance of their role, it is necessary to understand the relative paucity of musical provision in Wales at the turn of the century. As was usual in well-to-do families, the sisters received a good musical education, enough for Gwendoline to become an accomplished violinist. They had the wherewithal to travel and hear concerts outside Wales and the UK and attended the Bayreuth festival twice, in 1909 and 1911. These Wagner-saturated excursions, which excited in Margaret rhapsodic journal entries graphically documenting events (her favourite opera was *Siegfried*), were something of a musical pilgrimage. In addition to the operas and visiting Wahnfried, Wagner's home and grave, they visited the house of Hans Sachs, the central character in *Die Meistersinger*, and Liszt's grave.

Back in Wales, however, musical development had somewhat stagnated, largely because of patchy provision throughout the country. The indigenous choral tradition, on which the 'Land of Song' reputation was built, remained strong but, for many, music and chapel were inextricably linked. While there were brass bands in some areas, there was no national orchestra and instrumental provision in schools and, to an extent, universities was insufficient. There was, in addition, some resentment towards English composers and conductors, who the Welsh musical establishment saw as increasingly high-handed and meddling, looking to impose Germanic influence on local talent. Nevertheless, it was becoming evident to many that in addition to historic institutions such as the Eisteddfod and the ubiquity of the chapel, a broader, less insular approach was needed for the shaping of a new musical Wales.

Chapter opening: The chapter title comes from the foreword Gwendoline wrote in the programme for the 1935 Gregynog Festival, where she says 'let us fling out across the ether songs of glorious hope…'. The photograph shows Gustav Holst's signature on the score of the piece he composed especially for Gregynog. *Ray Edgar*

Right: Gwendoline playing the violin at Llandinam. Gwendoline had studied the violin in Paris, and for a time she owned a Stradivarius (the 'Parke'). However, she developed a rare blood disease that had a debilitating effect on her fingers and forced her to abandon her practice. *Private collection*

UNIVERSITY COLLEGE OF WALES MUSICAL CLUB.

SIXTH MEETING, TUESDAY, MAY 9TH, 1911.

Dr. ARTHUR SOMERVELL.
Violinist: Mr. EVAN WILLIAMS.

Part I.

1. VOCAL OCTETT—"The Dance" ... ... *Elgar*

   MISSES MATHER, LOVE, JONES, AND DAVIES,
   MESSRS. DAVIES, MORGAN, THOMAS, AND MASON.

2. CONCERTO in G minor for Violin ... *Max Bruch*

   MR. EVAN WILLIAMS.

3. (1) PART SONGS—
   (a) "Fairy Song" ... ... *Arthur Somervell*
   (b) "How sweet is the Shepherd's sweet lot" "

   GROUP OF COUNTY SCHOOL CHILDREN.

   (2) SOLOS—
   (a) "Night" ... ... *Arthur Somervell*
   (b) "My bed is a boat" ... "
   (c) "Dolly's Lullaby" ... "

   MISS MABLE PARRY.

   (3) DUET—"Two Doves on the selfsame branch"
   Arthur Somervell

   MISSES DORA ROWLANDS AND GWEN DAVIES.

4. CONCERTO in D minor for Piano and two Violins
   J. S. Bach

   MME. BARBIER,
   MESSRS. EVAN AND TOM WILLIAMS.

Part II.

1. VOCAL QUARTETS—
   (a) "Hope is like a harebell" *Arthur Somervell*
   (b) "Music, when soft voices die" "
   (c) "Going to bed" "
   (d) "When a mounting skylark sings" "
   (e) "High on the breakers" "

   MISSES DORA ROWLANDS AND GWEN DAVIES,
   MESSRS. DAVIES, TUDOR WILLIAMS, L. S. KNIGHT,
   AND JAMES.

2. SONATA in G major for Piano and Violin—
   Andante, Allegro ... *Haydn*

   MME. ANDRÉ BARBIER AND MR. EVAN WILLIAMS.

3. SONGS—
   (a) "She came to the village church" *Arthur Somervell*
   (b) "Birds in the high Hall-garden" ... "
   (c) "The fault was mine" ... ... "
   (d) "O that 'twere possible" ... ... "
   (e) "My life has crept so long" ... ... "

   MR. L. S. KNIGHT.

4. PIANOFORTE SOLO—Three Preludes *Arthur Somervell*
   (a) D♭; (b) F minor; (c) F major.

   THE COMPOSER.

5. SONGS—
   (a) "In the doorway" ... *Arthur Somervell*
   (b) "Dainty little maiden" ... "

   MME. ANDRÉ BARBIER.

6. VIOLIN SOLO—
   "Zigeunerweisen" ... ... *Sarasate*

   MR. EVAN WILLIAMS.

"HEN WLAD FY NHADAU"; "GOD SAVE THE KING."

The Davies sisters supported significant pockets of progressive musical activity occurring at the time. Despite their concerns about the state of contemporary Welsh music, their interest in the traditional music of Wales was strong as of course was their devotion to church and choral music. The mix of the sacred and secular, vernacular and cosmopolitan was to become a feature of the Gregynog festivals throughout the 1930s. The Welsh Folk-Song Society had been formed in 1908, and both sisters had sat on the general committee since 1909, taking an active role in its business – according to the society's journal, 'Miss Daisy Davies' had in 1910 offered a prize in Caersws for 'Collection of Folk-songs', and around 1916 both sisters had assisted Dr Mary Davies in collecting the folk songs of Montgomeryshire. The value they placed on vernacular music was illustrated in Margaret's Bayreuth journals, where she describes hearing in a German village 'a man with a very fine voice singing some of the German songs one knows so well … one could not have heard a better voice I think even in the opera house.'

Above: The programme for one of Madame Lucie Barbier's concerts at Aberystwyth, featuring Gwendoline and Dora Rowlands (later Herbert Jones) as performers. *Llyfrgell Genedlaethol Cymru - The National Library of Wales*

In other developments, under the direction of Madame Lucie Barbier, a University Music Club at Aberystwyth was established and between 1910 and 1915 audiences had the opportunity to hear performers of international repute playing not only French music such as Saint-Saëns and Franck, but madrigals, German *Lieder*, contemporary Welsh and English music and, importantly, Welsh folk song. Barbier also took a Welsh quartet to Paris, where they were, in the words of Dora Herbert Jones, 'like a glass of cold water' to the public. Taking an active role in the musical life of the country and (initially at least) as a friend of Barbier, Gwendoline featured as a performer in numerous concerts, including in 1910 as part of a vocal quartet singing the works of Arthur Somervell and in 1911 playing Svendsen's *Romance* and Dvořák's *Humoresque*. To be not only capable of playing these pieces, but of playing them in public, indicates that Gwendoline's skill was significantly greater than the average musical education of young ladies of the period.

Lasting musical change in Wales did not begin until 1914, when press reports of a large donation to fund a Chair of Music at Aberystwyth abounded. There were conflicting rumours of precisely how much was donated and by whom, but it was revealed to be 'Miss [Gwendoline] Davies who … has taken a keen interest and very practical steps in developing instrumental music, and fostering a love for it in Wales.' The donation, £3,000 a year for five years, was for proper musical provision at the University of Wales, but in fact it went far deeper than this. *The Welsh Outlook* reported that 'The wish was expressed by the donor that the staff should conduct concerts in suitable centres in Wales with a view to encouraging the formation of musical clubs and orchestral classes, and generally stimulate the study of good music.'

It was not until 1918 that the gift came into its own, and Thomas Jones and the sisters persuaded the Oswestry-born composer Henry Walford Davies to leave his London life and take up what he would later describe privately as 'the Welsh plough'. The sisters' donation funded his joint role as Chair of Music at Aberystwyth and Director of the newly formed National Council of Music, which had been set up to reform education and access to music throughout Wales.

Walford's task was, in many respects, thankless. Despite stout approval from reformers, to some his appointment seemed to be little more than external meddling, and there was opposition from musical nationalists who saw it as an attempt to impose a distinctly Germanic bias on Wales's stubbornly guarded sense of musical self. As Gwendoline noted in a letter to T.J., 'we have led the Welsh horse to the clearest brook we could possibly get, yet he has only tossed his head and walked right through'. Walford was more than able to stand up to those who accused him of pushing the European agenda at the expense of the local and he saw the absolute importance of both, noting that 'any conspiracy against variety is a crime. Any failure to set the highest possible value on home products is a crime.' He was deeply committed to the task in hand, and the tone of his writing – evident in personal journals, correspondence and professional reports – resounds with optimistic enthusiasm. His musical purpose was simple, reflected in these notes for the Aberystwyth Summer School of 1921: 'It must help' he wrote, 'if we all note at the outset that we all meet with three things in common in our minds about music:

> Somehow, we all <u>love</u> it
> Loving it, we somehow <u>make</u> it
> Making it, we <u>communicate</u> it to others'

Gwendoline and Walford Davies became close allies, possibly because they shared views not only on the intrinsic value of music, but also on its social and moral benefit and the need to democratize it. It can be argued that the Gregynog Festivals, far from democratizing music, were exclusive events where the social conscience was left on the collection plate at the door, but this is unfair when one considers the vast social range that Gregynog played host to during the rest of the year.

Despite resistance, and under the guidance of Walford Davies and the patronage of the Davies sisters, the National Council of Music transformed music provision in Wales in schools, universities and adult education. It undertook festivals, summer schools and concert-lectures and took Welsh music out of Wales. The sisters had put Gregynog at Walford's disposal, and Gregynog Press produced material to promote the events. The Council instigated a full-time string trio who travelled the country giving lecture concerts in rural areas to people whose only previous contact with music would have been through the church and chapel. The Council also produced a *Cymanfa Ganu* book in 1921 – for which the discussion notes reveal that responsibility for the selection of translations of Welsh hymns was given to Gwendoline and Dr Mary Davies. Gwendoline was also on the selection panel for a hymn tune book for schools and colleges.

Right: A charcoal portrait of Henry Walford Davies (1936), by Evan Walters. By all accounts, Walford Davies was a genial man who took the musical challenges he faced in Wales in his stride. This charcoal drawing by the Welsh artist Evan Walters captures the character of the sitter.

Next page, left: A poster for the performance of Haydn's *The Creation* at Aberystwyth in 1925. The National Council of Music enabled many local festivals, some of which still occur today. This original artwork for a performance of Haydn's *The Creation* was produced by Robert Ashwin Maynard at the Gregynog Press. *University of Wales, Gregynog*

Next page, right: A poster for the Welsh Week at Wembley. Walford Davies organized Welsh Week at Wembley in 1924 as a means of promoting the work of the National Council of Music outside Wales and 'fitting the best interests of music in Wales.' This poster was designed at the Gregynog Press. *University of Wales, Gregynog*

Evan Walters

GWYL GERDDOROL CEREDIGION
CARDIGANSHIRE
MUSICAL FESTIVAL

1723 : HAYDN : 1809

"THE CREATION"

AT THE

COLLEGE HALL
ABERYSTWYTH
FRIDAY MAY 29TH
"1925"

WELSH WEEK AT WEMBLEY AUG. 25-30

Y DDRAIG GOCH DDYRY GYCHWYN

MESSIAH · APOSTLES · CHURCH MUSIC
GERONTIUS · SYMPHONY ORCHESTRA
PASSION MUSIC · PENILLION SINGING
HYMN SINGING · WELSH GUARDS BAND

AN ALL WALES CHOIR AT THE STADIUM SATURDAY AUG. 30

IS YOUR CHOIR REPRESENTED? APPLY SECRETARY NATIONAL COUNCIL OF MUSIC ABERYSTWYTH

Designed by R.A. MAYNARD at The GREGYNOG PRESS Montgomeryshire

WATERLOW & SONS Lᵗᵈ LONDON DUNSTABLE & WATFORD

The importance of Gregynog as a location for the sisters' artistic and philanthropic pursuits is described elsewhere in this book, and its use as a musical centre was no different. Various plans – including making it a centre for music in Wales – did not come to fruition, neither did Gwendoline's vision of 'extending glass roofing across the stableyard and you have a workshop, concert hall, theatre, exhibition hall and Crystal Palace all in one', (though part of the yard did indeed receive a glass awning). Yet as a base for Walford Davies, a meeting place for the National Council of Music and venue for numerous concerts, conferences and other musical events during the 1920s and 1930s, the Hall received many eminent musical visitors including Elgar and Vaughan Williams, and saw performances by groups such as the English Singers (whose visit is thought to have inspired the formation of the Gregynog Choir). The billiard room became the Music Room, of which the Gregynog organ – built between 1922 and 1925 to Walford's specifications – was the centre-piece.

As a natural progression, the widely acclaimed Gregynog Choir – made up of staff members and local people – was formed in 1929, a solution to the problem of church attendance during conferences. Although it is apocryphal that the ability to sing was a requirement for employment at the Hall, there are certainly instances of individuals being supported financially because of their musical ability. As most of the choir members could not read staff notation, the tonic sol-fa system was favoured, and those who could not read tonic sol-fa learned parts by ear.

Music at Gregynog reached a peak in the 1930s with the advent of the Gregynog Festival of Music and Poetry, which ran annually from 1933 to 1938, and then again from 1955. It was a relatively small three or four day affair, by invitation only, with concerts taking place in the 200-seat Music Room and collections taken for local causes. The poetry element was considered just as important as the music, having 'an equal place in her own right at the side of the sister and familiar art.' During the 1930s, the festivals played host to some of the most important musical figures of the period including Gustav Holst, the conductor Adrian Boult and performers such as Jelly d'Arányi and the Rothschild Quartet. Boult became a regular feature, as did the acclaimed singers Elsie Suddaby and Keith Falkner. The pattern and programme of each Festival was always similar, comprising contemporary British music (Holst, Vaughan Williams and Elgar all featured heavily) and the not-so-contemporary (Arne, Boyce, Purcell and English Madrigalists) as well as a smattering of European chamber classics and a strong Welsh folk song element. Naturally, choral music dominated and religious works were programmed for Sundays.

In keeping with the holistic nature of the Festivals, the Gregynog Press produced special programmes for the event. It was, in many respects, a chamber festival – apart from ambitious

choral works, instrumentalists were few, and where a full orchestra would have been necessary, the relevant parts were filled by Walford Davies or Boult on the piano and organ. Despite the international flavour of the performers, there was an important Welsh emphasis, with many local musicians participating as well as, of course, the Gregynog Choir. At the first festival, Dora Herbert Jones gave a performance entitled 'Wales, her history and folk-music', with songs and a lecture. One of the most important Gregynog premieres was Holst's *O Spiritual Pilgrim* (with the dedication 'For Gregynog'), based on a poem by James Elroy Flecker and composed especially for the Gregynog Choir. Holst completed the short, unaccompanied choral work in 1933 after he attended the first Gregynog Festival, but died in May 1934 a few weeks before the first performance was given at the 1934 Festival.

Above: The Gregynog Choir on the steps of the Welsh Calvinist Methodist Chapel on the Charing Cross Road in London. This photograph was taken to commemorate the Royal Command Performance at the Albert Hall on Empire Day 1938. It was a large event featuring massed choirs from across the UK, designed to 'encourage music-making, and to benefit musicians in need'. The Gregynog Choir gave the first public performance of Holst's *O Spiritual Pilgrim*, under the direction of their regular conductor, W. R. Allen (front, third from left). *University of Wales, Gregynog*

Above: The Gregynog Organ. The organ was built to Walford Davies's specifications by the organ maker Frederick Rothwell, with whom he had worked previously at both the Temple Church and Windsor. Begun in 1922 as a two-manual, the organ was twice extended, becoming a large three-manual by 1925. Gwendoline herself was a proficient organist and frequently accompanied the singing of Dora Herbert Jones. *University of Wales, Gregynog*

Right: Sir Adrian Boult with Lascelles Abercrombie. Sir Adrian Boult first visited Gregynog in 1925 when he was conducting the orchestra at the Montgomery County Music Festival and he returned many times to conduct the Gregynog Choir with whom he became associated. He is seen here (left) at Gregynog in the 1930s with the poet Lascelles Abercrombie, whose work was frequently performed at the Festivals. *Private collection*

Although the festival was responsible for showcasing new work from some of the most important British composers of the early twentieth century, there was nothing of the European avant-garde aside from a Kodály song-cycle in 1938 and, interestingly, no hint of Lucie Barbier's French-based Aberystwyth programmes except for once in 1935 when the Rothschild Quartet played Ravel's *String Quartet in F*. The absence of the avant-garde is perhaps not such a surprise, for when the Hungarian Bartók had visited Aberystwyth in 1922 to give a concert, Walford Davies had afterwards apparently been heard to comment 'Baffling, isn't it?' It was not until the 1950s that names such as Stravinsky crept into concert programmes at Gregynog, but perhaps the most basic observation to be made on this musical conservatism – with a knowledge of the sisters' ideals – is that the Festival's purpose was not to challenge the listener but to comfort, inspire and uplift. A quite astonishing foreword, clearly by Gwendoline, in the programme of the 1935 festival seems to reflect the growing unrest in Europe and the idea of Gregynog as a type of haven:

> Is there no one who will call a halt to destruction?
> No imaginative mind which through our swiftly growing
> knowledge will reveal anew the wisdom of the eternities?
> Shall we not fill the world with beauty once again?
> Cheating despair, let us fling out across the ether songs of
> glorious hope and courage, till the sound-laden air is so charged
> with beauty that there is no room for despair!

The addition to the programme of compositions by the recently deceased Peter Warlock (a concert in1932 and the Festival in 1936) raises some interesting questions. The composer died in 1930. Between 1921 and 1924 he lived largely at his family home at Abermule, barely seven miles from Tregynon, yet he was apparently never invited to Gregynog. It is possible, as has been suggested by more than one source, that his bohemian reputation and purported links to the occult would render him *persona non grata* at the sober Hall. Ironically, his exquisite, jewel-like songs – which took their cue from the Elizabethan and with a strong poetry element – slotted seamlessly into the programme at Gregynog.

Right: Dora Herbert Jones. Dora Herbert Jones became a friend of Gwendoline at Aberystwyth and later worked with the sisters in their war-time canteen in France. A talented and respected singer, her reputation was principally as an exponent of Welsh folk song. Her input into the cultural life at Gregynog was considerable – in 1927 she became secretary to both the sisters and the Gregynog Press, and later became choral secretary and librarian to the Gregynog Choir, working alongside Henry Walford Davies to develop the musical reputation of the Hall. *Llyfrgell Genedlaethol Cymru - The National Library of Wales*

THE THIRD FESTIVAL

OF

MUSIC & POETRY

to be held at
GREGYNOG
June 28th-July 1st
1935

Contributions in aid
of the Orthopaedic Hospital and Derwen
Cripples Training College Oswestry
will be accepted

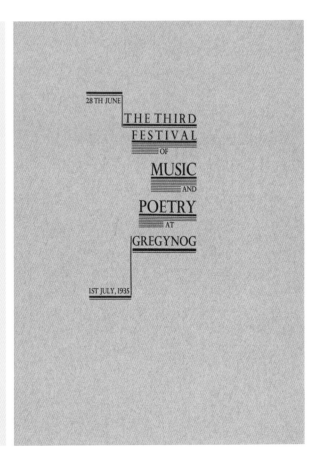

Previous pages: A manuscript score of *O Spiritual Pilgrim*. Holst had intended to dedicate the work to Dora Herbert Jones, whom he greatly admired and who sang for him on numerous occasions. However, she persuaded him to dedicate it to the choir instead, though the more ambiguous dedication 'For Gregynog' was eventually used. *Llyfrgell Genedlaethol Cymru - The National Library of Wales*

Above: The programme produced by Gregynog Press for the Third Festival of Music and Poetry in 1935.

Right: The score of Vaughan Williams's *Toward the Unknown Region* in a Gregynog Press binding, designed by William McCance and presented to Sir Adrian Boult at the First Gregynog Festival of Music and Poetry.

The advent of war in 1939 halted musical activity at Gregynog, and the Festivals ceased as the sisters turned their attention to the war effort. The death of Walford Davies in 1941, and of Gwendoline ten years later, had a profound effect on the musical life of Gregynog, and though plans were mooted to transform the Hall into a centre for Welsh music, these never came to fruition. At the Gregynog Conference of 1952 there was talk of the establishment of a Composers' Guild, Margaret suggesting the venue as 'a quiet retreat for persons wishing to compose music'. The scheme was cancelled in 1954 owing to staffing difficulties, although many Guild for the Promotion of Welsh Music activities centred around Gregynog in the 1950s. At his appointment to the post of Gregynog Professor of Music at Aberystwyth, Ian Parrott resurrected the musical spirit of the Hall by reviving the Festival in 1955, and it ran until 1961, largely adhering to the ethos of the earlier programmes, but with a new emphasis on contemporary Welsh composers. In 1988, the Festival was revived again, this time by the tenor Anthony Rolfe Johnson, and it continues today under the direction of Dr Rhian Davies – a tangible example of the sisters' musical legacy in Wales.

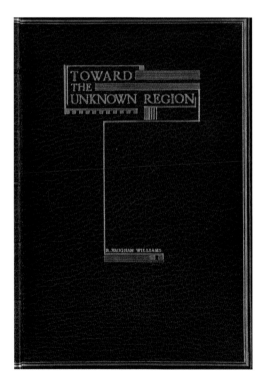

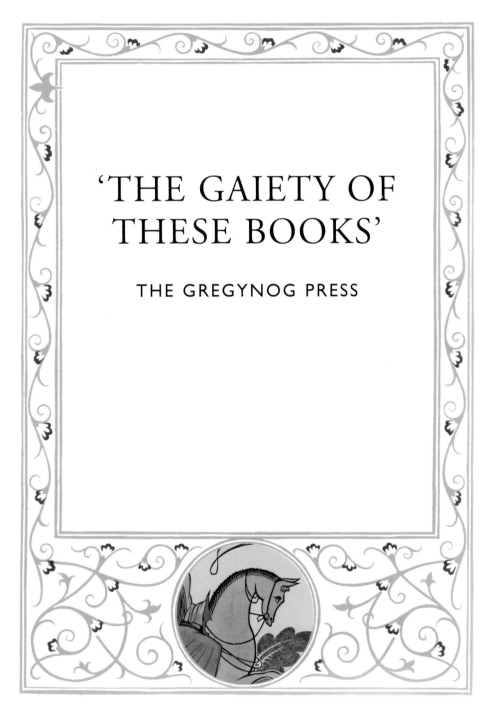

'THE GAIETY OF THESE BOOKS'

THE GREGYNOG PRESS

ONE OF THE outstanding aspects of the Davies sisters' involvement in the arts was the creation of the Gregynog Press. The prime aim of the Press was to 'help cultivate a love of beautiful things in the people of Wales by means of the practice of such arts and crafts as printing, binding [and] illustration'. However, its major impact was to be on the collectors of limited edition private press books and on those interested in the art of the fine book.

The Press became one of the most famous of its kind in the first half of the twentieth century, along with the Golden Cockerel Press. What makes these establishments different when compared to mainstream publishing is that they are generally small, private concerns, printing fine books by hand on hand-made paper. Gregynog first used an Albion Press, although a Victoria platen press was soon acquired.

Of the two sisters, it was Gwendoline who was the closest in the furtherance of the aims and aspirations of the Press, but the sisters' library contained several private press books, including examples from the Kelmscott and Ashendene presses, now in the National Library of Wales. However, both kept their distance from the daily operations, relying on Thomas Jones, the Press Board's Chairman, to oversee matters, although the sisters were members of the board, which met in London and Gregynog. It was T.J. who played a key role in all matters relating to Gregynog and the Press, and who was instrumental in endeavouring to smooth what was at times a fraught relationship between the key personnel and the sisters, and it is generally recognized that without T.J. the Press would not have existed. From 1927, Dora Herbert Jones became full-time secretary to the Press.

Three aspects of the Press in particular differentiate it from other private presses. These were the publication of several titles in Welsh, the importance attached to the production of a limited edition of each title in a special binding and the fact that, in many instances, the artist was able to work alongside the printer to ensure complete unity between letterpress and wood-engraving.

From 1923 until it ceased book production in 1940, the Press published forty-two titles, with a further three issued for private circulation. It was also responsible for a large amount of ephemera such as book prospectuses, music festival programmes and orders of services, and it continued in this vein for a short period after 1940. The Gregynog Press did continue as a limited company until 1965, when it went into voluntary liquidation. Most of the equipment had

Chapter opening: The chapter's title is from *The Private Presses* by Colin Franklin. The photograph shows some the Press's lead type still in the case and still on view today at Gregynog.

been passed to the National Library of Wales in 1954, although shortly beforehand Iorwerth Peate, Curator of St Fagans, had tried to persuade T.J. to pass the Press to the Museum with an endowment, to continue printing.

Hugh Blaker, who had been advising the sisters on their art acquisitions since 1908, was the man to whom they and T.J. turned for advice regarding the appointment of a Controller at Gregynog, who was to oversee instruction in various crafts – for as originally envisaged, Gregynog was not just to be the home of a small press but a setting for a wide range of arts and crafts as well as a conference centre. Although it was hoped that the Controller would be Welsh, Blaker's recommendation, the artist Robert Ashwin Maynard, was appointed in February 1921. Until moving to Gregynog in July 1922, Maynard spent time in London receiving instruction in various aspects of arts and crafts. However, it was to be printing and engraving that most interested him. The first production from the Press was the Davies sisters'

Above: Robert Maynard's wood engraving of Montgomery Castle, printed in the first book published by the Press, George Herbert's *The poems of George Herbert*. This image is taken from Gwendoline's own copy. Her collection of the special bindings is on loan to the Museum from the Gwendoline and Margaret Davies charities.

Christmas card for 1922 featuring a wood-engraving of Gregynog and its surrounding land-scape by Maynard, and Christmas cards were produced each year until 1938.

The following year general assistants were appointed to work with Maynard, namely John Mason and John Hugh Jones, the former also taking on the role of bookbinder. However, 1923 was an important year for more than just the arrival of additional staff, for the first book was published at the end of that year. This was *The poems of George Herbert*, the selection of the poems having been undertaken by Henry Walford Davies. This modest book was well received in bibliographic circles. Maynard engraved in wood the illustration of Montgomery Castle and also the initial letters, which were printed in red. The ordinary edition was bound in cloth and marbled paper boards, the special editions mainly in crimson levant morocco. The book was printed on hand-made paper, and it was this quality of paper, including 'Japanese vellum', that was used for all the titles.

In early 1924 Horace Walter Bray joined the Press as resident artist. Among the other new staff was Idris Jones, who was to become the Press's printer in its twilight years. The second title was published, *Poems by Henry Vaughan*, as modest in size as the Herbert book with the poems chosen by the novelist and poet Ernest Rhys. Maynard prepared the initials once again, but both he and Bray were responsible for the thirteen wood-engravings.

The Maynard and Bray partnership at Gregynog lasted until 1930, when both men left to set up the Raven Press, with limited success. After the Vaughan poems, a further sixteen books were published and over sixty ephemeral publications. What turned out to be an outstanding appointment was the recruitment of George Fisher as the binder at the end of 1925. He stayed at the Press for twenty years, the longest serving member. Fisher saw himself as a craftsman, and although when he arrived at Gregynog he had not undertaken bookbinding for several years, his talent was soon recognized. He set high standards of work both for himself and his assistants. The special bindings were largely Fisher's work, and he even designed some of them.

Top, left: The special binding of Edward Thomas's *Chosen essays* (1926), designed by Robert Maynard, and one of the earliest examples of George Fisher's bindings.

Top, right: The special binding of *The life of Saint David* (1927), designed by Horace Bray and bound by George Fisher.

Bottom, left: One of the specially bound copies of the Loyal Address to King George V on the formal opening of the National Museum of Wales on 21 April 1927. This copy was signed by all the Officers of the Museum.

Bottom, right: The Museum's Library holds three copies of *Llyfr y Pregeth-wr* (1927), all bound differently. Gwen Davies's copy is one of four that were printed on vellum, each having a very decorative binding designed and executed by George Fisher. Of the other two, printed on hand-made paper, one is the ordinary edition bound in a blue buckram cloth, while the third is one of the less ornate special bindings, in dark blue levant morocco.

The third title to be published was the first in Welsh, *Caneuon Ceiriog detholiad* in 1925 while the seventh, *The life of Saint David* in 1927, was the first book to have colour added by hand, the wood-engravings being coloured by the female staff in the bindery under Bray's supervision. November 1927 was a landmark month for the Press as, besides the publication of *Saint David*, the first book with wood-engravings by an external artist appeared. This was *Llyfr y Pregeth-wr* ('the Book of Ecclesiastes'), with wood-engravings by the artist David Jones.

The life of Saint David and *Llyfr y Pregeth-wr* are notable for another reason: in 1927 Herbert John Hodgson joined as pressman or printer. Hodgson, who remained at the Press until 1936, was one of the great printers of fine books of the twentieth century, and these two titles were his first undertakings. That year also marked the formal opening of the Museum in April and, in spite of short notice, the Press agreed to print some of the copies of the Loyal Address used at the opening. The final two full years of Maynard and Bray (1928-9) saw the publication of the first folio volume, *The autobiography of Edward Lord Herbert of Cherbury*, and one of the most decorated books, *Psalmau Dafydd*, based on the text in the William Morgan Bible of 1588. *Edward Lord Herbert* received fulsome praise from notices in the national press and book collectors. *Psalmau Dafydd* was one of the most popular books produced by the Press, and its two hundred copies were quickly subscribed to.

Before Maynard and Bray's departure an edition of Christina Rossetti's poems appeared, and a copy was exhibited in the British Museum in a display of the fifty best books of that year. However, this was not the final product of their successful Gregynog partnership, for other titles were in various stages of production and appeared later in 1930 and in 1931, and Maynard returned to oversee production. This output included the two-volume *Elia*, which had been completed in late 1929 and early 1930, and contains some of the finest wood-engravings that Bray undertook. One of the most handsome productions of this partnership was *The stealing of the mare*, with its glorious gold and hand-coloured frontispiece and initial letters.

The Board turned once again to Hugh Blaker for advice on a replacement Controller. The man proposed was Blair Hughes-Stanton, but he preferred the post of artist, and so it was William McCance who succeeded Maynard. The wives of McCance and Hughes-Stanton, respectively Agnes Miller Parker and Gertrude Hermes, were paid a retainer to undertake engravings for the Press. Thus was ushered in the golden era at Gregynog, certainly in terms of book illustration,

Right, top: The wood engravings for *The life of Saint David* (1927) were undertaken by Robert Maynard and Horace Bray and hand-coloured by staff in the bindery.

Right, bottom: A wood engraving by David Jones from *Llyfr y Pregeth-wr* (1927).

AT this time well nigh the third or fourth part of Ireland was subject unto David the Waterman. There Maeddog was, who also from his infancy was known as Aeddan, to whom St. David gave the little bell, which was called "Cruedin." But when sailing to Ireland Aeddan forgot his bell. And he sent a messenger to holy David that he might send his beloved little bell back to him. And Saint David said, "Go, boy, again to thy master." And lo! the little bell on the morrow was safe in the hand of the good Aeddan, for an Angel bore it across the sea before the boy he sent for it had come thither.

AFTER that time it was that Modomnoc, having served David with humility for many years, took ship and sailed over to Ireland. Now Modomnoc had attended to

the beehives of the Monastery in Vallis Rosina, and when he went down to the ship, behold a swarm of bees followed him, & settled where he sat in the ship's prow. But he, unwilling to take them from the brethren of the Monastery returned with

them, and came again to Saint David, while they swarmed around him & then flew back to their old beehives. And David blessed him for that humble service. And again, bidding farewell to the father and his brethren, Modomnoc started on his journey & again the bees followed him. And so it was, yet a second, and a third time. And at the third time Saint David told Modomnoc to take them also. Then David spoke to the bees and blessed them, saying: "May the land, O bees, to which you go, abound with your offspring. Never may your children be wanting within its shores. For now our own sacred close shall be deserted by you for ever, and your offspring shall no more grow up among us. Go in peace!" And since that time, as is well known, the island of Ireland is enriched with great store of honey.

GWAGEDD o WAGEDD

medd y Pregeth-wr, gwagedd o wagedd, gwagedd yw'r cwbl. Pa fudd sydd i ddyn oi hôll lafur, a gymmero efe dann yr haul? Un genhedlaeth a aiff ymmaith, a chenhedlaeth arall a ddaw: ond y ddaiar a saif byth. Yr haul hefyd a gyfŷd, a't haul a fachluda, ac a dynn iw le, lle y mae yn codi. Efe a aiff i't dehau, ac a amgylcha i't gogledd: y mae't gwynt yn myned oddi amgylch, ac yn dychwelyd yn ei gwmpas. Yr hôll afonydd a rêdant i't môr, ac etto nid yw't môr yn llawn: i ba le bynnac y rhêdo't afonydd oddi yno y dychwêlant eil-waith. Pôb peth sydd yn llawn blinder, ni ddichon nêb ei dreuthu: ni chaiff y llygad ddigon o edrych, na't glûst o wrando. Y pêth a fu a fydd, a't peth a wnaed a wnêir, ac nid oes dim newydd dann yr haul. A oes dim y gellir dywedyd, edrych at hwn, dymma beth newydd: canys efe fu yn yr hên amser o'n blaen ni. Nid oes goffa am y pethau gynt, ac ni bydd coffa am y pethau a ddaw yn ôl, gan y rhai a ddaw ar eu hôl hwynt. Myfi y Pregeth-wr oeddwn frenin Israêl yn Ierusalem: Ac a roddais fy mrŷd ar geisio, ac ar chwilio am ddoethineb, am bôb peth a wnaed tann y nefoedd: dymma drafael flin a roddes Duw ar feibion dynnion i ymguro ynddi. Mi a welais yr holl weithredoedd y rhai sydd tann haul, a wele y rhai hynny ôll ydynt wagedd a gorthrymder yspryd.

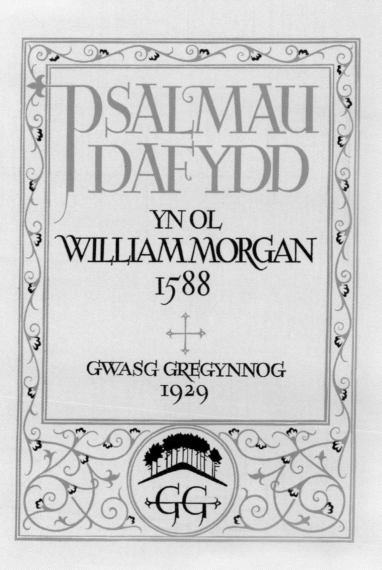

PSALMAU DAFYDD

YN OL
WILLIAM MORGAN
1588

✠

GWASG GREGYNNOG
1929

for Miller Parker and Hughes-Stanton were two of the finest wood-engravers of the twentieth century. The former went on to undertake numerous commissions in the 1940s and 1950s for commercial publishers. The Gregynog books for which they produced engravings are amongst the most sought after volumes by collectors. It is unfortunate that McCance's *Book of Job* and an edition of Gilbert White's *Selborne*, with engravings by Hermes, were never published by the Press (although the six completed engravings for *Selborne* were issued later by Gwasg Gregynog in 1988). The time spent at Gregynog by these four was not particularly happy for both personal and work-related reasons, and the Board was concerned about some of Hughes-Stanton's erotic engravings. Engravings for W. H. Davies's *The lovers' song-book* by first Hughes-Stanton and then Hermes were rejected, and the book did not appear until late in 1933, unillustrated and among the least attractive of the Press's output.

The first McCance/Hughes-Stanton book was John Milton's *Comus*, published in September 1931. This book and two from the Maynard/Bray period were among those exhibited in the 1932 exhibition *Fifty best books of 1931*. *Comus* was arranged by McCance, with Hughes-Stanton assisting in the printing and design as well providing the eight engravings. Hughes-Stanton also designed the special binding, a very handsome production in dun-coloured levant morocco; one of the notable aspects of the partnership of these two men was the beautifully crafted designs of some of the special bindings. Hughes-Stanton went on to design a total of six special editions, three of which were commissions after he had left Gregynog, while McCance designed two. Among the 1932 publications was *The fables of Esope*, with Miller Parker's numerous engravings, the ordinary edition bound in full Welsh sheepskin and the specials in a more ornate levant morocco designed by McCance. He also designed another special that year, Robert Vansittart's *The singing caravan*, the binding having an intricate pattern of gold lines and a fore-edge flap in oriental style.

Nineteen thirty-three was a momentous year for the Press. Both McCance and Hughes-Stanton left in September, and thereafter there was no Controller in residence, nor an artist. Two of the greatest Gregynog books were produced, although one was not issued until the following year. These were *The revelation of Saint John the Divine* and *The lamentations of Jeremiah*, designed and illustrated by Hughes-Stanton. He also designed the special bindings, arguably Fisher's greatest work. Also, Hodgson's skill as the printer greatly enhanced the aesthetic quality of these books. John Sampson's collection of *XXI Welsh gypsy folk-tales* also appeared, with wood-engravings by Agnes Miller Parker.

Left: The title page of *Psalmau Dafydd* (1929) - and the inspiration for the decorative motifs used with our chapter titles.

The American Loyd Haberly was persuaded to become the part-time Controller of the Press from the beginning of 1934, Dora Herbert Jones having overseen the daily running since the previous September. Haberly resigned after two years, and James Wardrop of the Victoria and Albert Museum became part-time Controller in the summer of 1936, Thomas Jones having had great difficulty in finding a replacement for Haberly. Soon after the outset of the Second World War, Wardrop stepped down from the position. The final Gregynog Press book was *Lyrics and unfinished poems*, written by Lascelles Abercrombie, a frequent visitor to Gregynog, and published in August 1940.

Following the departure of McCance and Hughes-Stanton the Press produced a further fourteen titles, with an additional two issued for private circulation. Several have notable features, but none is comparable to the best of the Press's early 1930s' output. *Eros and Psyche* (1935) was the first and only book to be printed using the new Gregynog type. *Cyrupaedia* (1936) is regarded as the best book published during Haberly's time, especially with the use of hand-coloured initials. Fisher's binding of this book was to a design by Lady Cartwright of Aynho, and is one of the least attractive of the specials, while the ordinary by Bowen, his assistant, in full green oasis with decorative onlays, is aesthetically the finer design.

The story of a red-deer (1935/6) was the only book produced at Gregynog where the illustrations were printed in colour. For Greville's *Caelica* (1937) Hughes-Stanton designed the special binding, while Wardrop and his wife Evelyn were responsible for the ordinary binding. Also in 1937 the Press published *The history of Saint Louis*, a work with which a number of artists were involved. This is generally regarded not only as the best example of Wardrop's output at Gregynog, but as a book that contains one of the finest examples of an opening page of any printed. In the following year the Press published a delightful little work, Guevara's *The praise and happinesse of countrie-life*, with engravings by Reynolds Stone.

One of the few titles where the ordinary binding excelled over the special was George Bernard Shaw's *Shaw gives himself away* (1939). The artist Paul Nash was invited to design the bindings, Gwendoline Davies herself having rejected the Fisher and Wardrop design. However, only Nash's work for the ordinary was used, which had orange onlays (derived from Shaw's initials) on dark green oasis, with Fisher producing a new design for the specials.

Some negative comments have been made about the Gregynog Press: the output of the Press was small, and it cannot be said to have achieved all of its original aims. Nevertheless, the best

Right: The frontispiece to *The stealing of the mare* (1930), the work of Robert Maynard.

The SECOND FABLE *is of the auncyent* WESEL *and of the* RAT:

YTTE IS BETTER THAN force or ſtrengthe: As reherceth to vs this fable of an old weſel: the whiche myghte no more take no rats: wherfore ſhe was ofte ſore hongry and bethought her that ſhe ſhold hyde her ſelf with-ymme the flowre for to take the rats whiche came there for to ete hit: And as the rats came to the floure: ſhe took and ete them eche one after other: And as the oldeſt rat of all perceyued & knewe her malyce: he ſayd thus in hym ſelf: Certaynly I ſhalle kepe me wel fro the: For I knowe alle thy malyce & falſhede ℭ And therfore he is wyſe that ſcapeth the wytte and malyce of euylle folke: by wytte and not by force

The THIRDE FABLE *is of the* WULF *and of* the SHEEPHERD *and of the* HUNTER

ANY FOLKE SHEWE them-ſelf good by theyr wordes whiche are ful of grete fantaſyes: As re-hercceth to vs thys fable of a wulf whiche fledde byfore the hunter: and as he fledde he mette with a ſheepherd: to whome he ſaid my frende I praye the that thow telle not to hym that foloweth me whiche wey I am gone: & the ſheep herd ſaid to hym haue no drede ne fere nothynge: For I ſhalle not accuſe the: For I ſhalle ſhewe to hym another way:

And as the hunter came: he demaunded of the ſheepherd yf he had ſene the wulf paſſe: And the hunter both with the heed and the eyen ſhewed to the hunter the place where the wulf was: & with the hand and the tongue ſhewed alle the contrarye: And incontynent the hunter vnderſtood hym wel: But the wulf whiche perceyued wel all the fayned maners of the ſheepherd fled awey: ℭ And within a lytyl whylle after the ſheepherd encountred and mette with the wulf: to whome he ſayd: paye me of that I haue kepte the ſecrete: ℭ And thenne the wulf anſuered to hym in this maner: I thanke thyn handes and thy tongue: and not thyn hede ne thyn eyen: For by them I ſhold haue ben betrayed: yf I had not fledde aweye: ℭ And therfore men muſt not truſte in hym that hath two faces and two tongues: for ſuche folk is lyke and ſemblable to the ſcorpion: the whiche enoynteth with his tongue: and prycketh ſore with his taylle

The FOURTH FABLE *is of* IUNO THE GODDESSE *and of the* PECOK *and of the* NYGHTYNGALE

VERY ONE OUGHTE TO BE content of kynde: and of ſuche good as god hath ſente vnto hym: wherof he muſt vſe ſuftly: As reherceth this fable of a pecok whiche came to Iuno the goddeſſe: and ſayd to her I am heuy and ſorowful: by cauſe I can not ſynge as wel as the nyghtyngale: by cauſe I can not ſynge: And one mocketh and ſcorneth me: And Iuno would comforte hym and ſayd: thy fayre forme and beaute is fayrer and more worthy and of gretter preyſynge than the ſonge of the nyghtryngale: For thy fethers and thy colour

A MASK BY JOHN MILTON

WITH
A FRONTISPIECE AND
THE SIX CHARACTERS IN
COSTUME DESIGNED AND
ENGRAVED ON WOOD BY
BLAIR HUGHES-STANTON

THE GREGYNOG PRESS
MCMXXXI

of the titles published during the controllership of Maynard and McCance rightly take their place among the finest books published in the twentieth century. This tradition in Wales of fine printing and binding has continued from the 1970s with the Press's heir, Gwasg Gregynog.

The Press is unique among the sisters' cultural enterprises in that their personal participation was quite limited. Although Margaret was a competent wood-engraver herself, she seems to have had little to do with the Press's artists. Some in the quiet Tregynon community also found the 'Press Gang', as they were sometimes called, alarmingly Bohemian. Nevertheless, the Press was very much part of the experience of Gregynog between the wars. Visitors to the house were usually shown the Press and their names are recorded in its visitors' book. Its ephemera mirror the sweep of life at Gregynog, and its books echo the sisters' desire to create, in music and the visual arts, something of beauty that was also distinctively Welsh.

Acknowledgements
The writer would like to thank David Vickers at Gwasg Gregynog for his assistance, but the greatest debt is owed to Dorothy Harrop's book on the Gregynog Press, without which this chapter could not have been written.

Left, top: *The fables of Esope* (1932). Agnes Miller Parker's wood engravings for this book, and *XXI Welsh gypsy folk-tales* (1933), established her position in the public eye as one of the greatest wood-engravers of the twentieth century. The book was published to wide acclaim, the Printer to Cambridge University Press informing Thomas Jones that he had never seen such a 'beautifully printed book'.

Left, bottom: The title page and frontispiece of Milton's *Comus* (1931), the first book from the McCance/Hughes-Stanton partnership, which ushered in the golden era of the Press in terms of illustration and fine binding design.

Above: One of the pages from *The story of the red-deer* (1935/6), a children's book, which was the last book produced by Loyd Haberly as Controller of the Press.

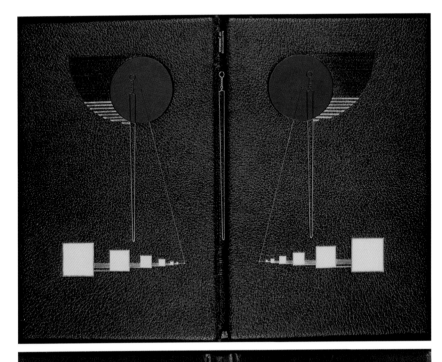

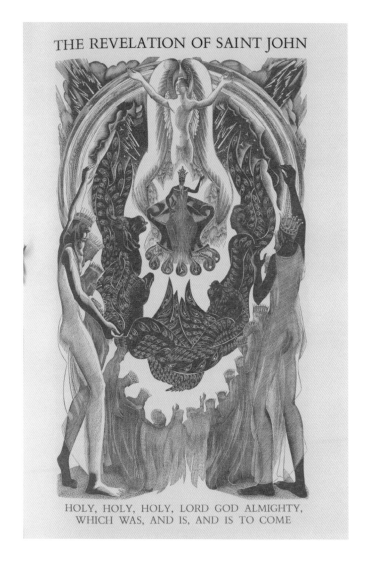

THE REVELATION OF SAINT JOHN

HOLY, HOLY, HOLY, LORD GOD ALMIGHTY,
WHICH WAS, AND IS, AND IS TO COME

Left, top: The special binding by George Fisher of *The lamentations of Jeremiah* (1933), to the design of Blair Hughes-Stanton.

Left, bottom: The ordinary binding of *Shaw gives himself away* (1939), designed by Paul Nash with orange onlays, based on George Bernard Shaw's initials, on a dark green oasis.

Above: Pages from *The revelation of Saint John the Divine* (1933), with some of the dramatic, almost erotic, wood-engravings by Blair Hughes-Stanton. The artist's work was very different in style to Miller Parker's engravings, but his engravings are technically brilliant, and the effect on the page emphasizes the quality of the printing by Herbert Hodgson.

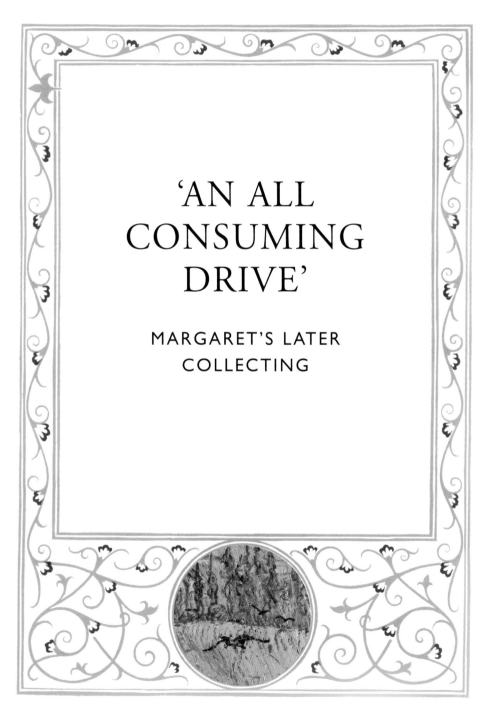

'AN ALL CONSUMING DRIVE'

MARGARET'S LATER COLLECTING

I T IS WITHOUT doubt the Impressionist and Post-Impressionist works of art now in the Welsh national collection for which Margaret Davies is best known. However, unlike her sister, Margaret continued to collect throughout her life (her last purchase was made in 1962, the year before her death) and her bequest of modern British pictures also forms an important, but less well-known, part of the Museum's collection.

Although the sisters bought individually, they saw the collection as one. Margaret's later collecting may have filled some of the gaps at Gregynog, but it is also likely that it took place with the Museum's existing collection of modern British art in mind. As such, the role of her advisers and the significance of her personal taste with regard to her collecting deserve further exploration.

Both Gwendoline and Margaret continued to buy art in the immediate aftermath of the First World War. In fact, it was during this time that they made some of their best-known and most expensive acquisitions. In March 1920, Gwendoline bought her third great canvas by Cézanne, *Still Life with Teapot*, and a month later acquired Van Gogh's outstanding late painting *Rain – Auvers*. Meanwhile, Margaret bought work by Pissarro, Vlaminck and Dérain. Although they continued to acquire paintings by established favourites such as Turner, Boudin, Daumier, Carrière and Augustus John, from 1919 to 1923 they also purchased a number of Old Master paintings including two Renaissance Madonnas after Botticelli. One of these works, a Dutch seventeenth-century portrait of a woman, was bought from Hugh Blaker for £9,000 and was one of the most expensive paintings they ever acquired.

Gwendoline stopped collecting in 1926 (her last acquisition was a landscape by Richard Wilson), redirecting her energies (and money) towards other more philanthropic causes. She wrote to Thomas Jones of the difficulty of buying work 'in the face of the appalling needs everywhere … after all it is humanity that needs help and sympathy'. Despite the economic hardships that had distracted her sister, as Margaret continued to paint, so she continued to collect, apart from a short break from 1927 to 1934. After this pause, her focus altered and she largely abandoned European art, which she had previously favoured, for modern British art.

When Margaret resumed collecting and was acquiring modern British art, she was doing so as a private collector. For the most part, the purposes of private and public collections are not so

Chapter opening: Vanessa Bell, *Dahlias and Canterbury Bells*. Purchased by Margaret from the Redfern Gallery in 1937. © The Estate of Vanessa Bell, courtesy of Henrietta Garnett

Right: A photograph of Margaret Davies, probably taken when she was in her late 60s. Margaret continued to collect art up until her death in 1963. Her last purchases included *Mornington Crescent* by Spencer Gore and *Landscape with Bonfire* by Oskar Kokoshka. *Private collection*

different. Both exist for inspiration, learning and enjoyment. However, museums are charged with safeguarding and making accessible artefacts for the public, and it is primarily the process of acquisition that varies. When buying for a private collection, the constraints are personal ones – for example, taste, preference, space and financial restrictions. Public institutions are supported by public money and are therefore subject to specific collecting policies and strategies. Collecting is arguably more methodical; objective decisions are made about individual works and artists, and their relevance to the existing collection and their historical importance have to be considered.

The education in art history that the Davies sisters received in 1907-8 was wide-ranging but did not include tutoring on many contemporary artists, and those that they studied were all well-established and not part of the current avant-garde. For example, Rodin was sixty-eight and acknowledged as one of the day's great sculptors. The sisters gained further knowledge over the years from advisers and literature, but Margaret's taste arguably became the more forward-thinking of the two. Her bequest was larger and more wide-ranging than Gwendoline's, partly because she collected for longer. It comprised 108 paintings, forty-two works on paper and one sculpture. Margaret's bequest is also more diffuse, with fewer widely celebrated artists, indeed it includes several who are almost unknown, though it would be wrong to conclude that the work is not of quality. Margaret made some adventurous purchases and, although she took advice, her own judgement remained prevalent. In 1924 Gwendoline wrote of the importance of the collector's personal taste and opinions, 'the great love of collecting is to do it yourself – with expert opinion, granted, but one does like to choose for oneself. All the time we have been collecting our pictures we have never bought one without having seen it or at least a photograph before purchase'. This philosophy remained relevant throughout Margaret's life.

In addition to modern British art, Margaret also began to focus on work by Welsh artists, possibly as a means of encouraging the production of art in Wales. At the time she began collecting again in the early 1930s, there was an increased desire among the arts community to raise public awareness of contemporary art in Wales. The most important development was the establishment of the Contemporary Art Society for Wales in 1935; both Davies sisters were present at the inaugural meeting and in 1954 Margaret became purchaser for the Society. During these years Margaret bought work for her own collection by Kyffin Williams, Cedric Morris, J. D. Innes, Esther Grainger, Josef Herman and Edward Morland Lewis among others. Of artists working in England, she bought work by Harold Gilman, Walter Sickert, Ronald Ossary Dunlop and Vanessa Bell. As with her earlier collecting, she consulted on purchases and one of her main advisors after Blaker's death was Murray Urquhart, a fellow artist and long-time family friend whose work Margaret also acquired.

Margaret retained the freedom afforded to private collectors and was more able to take risks with her purchases, which public collections are often reluctant to do. Of modern British artists, she bought work by Stanley Spencer, John Piper, Paul Nash (including his drawings of Gregynog, produced from his stay with the sisters in 1938) and John Nash. The lack of comprehensive 'groups' of painters in Margaret's collection further suggests that she was buying according to her taste. For example, although she owned work by Walter Sickert, Harold Gilman, Spencer Gore and Percy Wyndham Lewis from the Camden Town Group, she did not seek to buy work by any other members. This is also true of dominant groups such as Bloomsbury and St Ives, where only one or two individual artists were represented.

Although some of the pictures she bought were not by well-known 'names', many are. For example, Margaret bought work by Cedric Morris before national institutions such as the Tate, and other artists including Ivon Hitchens and Terry Frost were bought contemporaneously with the Tate (in fact at this point the Tate were only acquiring these works in single or low numbers; their collections were expanded much later). In a similar way, Margaret's policy for the most part was to buy one work by an artist. She did not seek to illustrate various aspects of their practice, simply to represent them. This also extended to her few late purchases of European art – she bought the only Alfred Sisley in the two bequests, a Henri Moret, Pierre Bonnard, Maurice

Above: Vincent van Gogh, *Rain – Auvers* (1890). Bought by Gwendoline in the immediate aftermath of the First World War in April 1920 for £2,020.

153

Following pages:

Percy Wyndham Lewis, *Ezra Pound*, around 1921. Purchased by Margaret from the Leicester Galleries in 1921 for £32 11d. Wyndham Lewis was a member of the Camden Town group of artists, which was founded by Sickert in 1911. Named after the seedy area in which Sickert had lived in north London, this group of British Post-Impressionists painted urban and landscape scenes in a variety of styles. Although Margaret did not seek to represent particular artistic movements in her collection she owned work by several members of the Camden Town group. © *Wyndham Lewis and the Estate of Mrs G. A. Wyndham Lewis by kind permission of the Wyndham Lewis Memorial Trust (a registered charity)*

Paul Nash, *Gregynog*, 1938. Bought by Margaret from the Leicester Galleries in 1957 for £157 10d. Nash visited the sisters at Gregynog in 1938 and drew and photographed the grounds during his stay there. © *Tate*

Pierre Bonnard, *Sunlight at Vernon*. Purchased by Margaret in 1960 from Roland, Browse and Delbanco for £14,700. This was one of the last European works to enter the collection and is the only work by Bonnard either of the sisters bought. It also remains the most expensive painting they purchased. © *ADAGP, Paris and DACS, London 2007*

Stanley Spencer, *Hilda Spencer*, 1947. Purchased by Margaret in 1960 from Arthur Tooth & Sons Ltd for £150. This is a portrait of Spencer's first wife and fellow artist Hilda Carline, whom he married in 1925 and divorced in 1937. It is the only work by Spencer in the sisters' collection. © *The Estate of Stanely Spencer/DACS 2007*

Cedric Morris, *Near Cagnes*. Purchased by Margaret from the Leicester Galleries in 1952 for £78 15d. Morris was an influential Welsh artist who, with his partner and fellow-artist Arthur Lett-Haines, set up the East Anglian School of Painting and Drawing. Their students included Lucian Freud and Maggie Hambling. © *The Esate of Sir Cedric Morriss*

Edouard Manet, *Boats – Argenteuil*, 1874. Margaret bought this study in Paris in 1920. It shows sailing boats in the foreground, laundry boats on the far side of the river and, in the distance, smoke rising from the tannery factories, for which Argenteuil was famous.

Terry Frost, *Brown Harbour*, around 1950. Purchased by Margaret from the Waddington Galleries in 1961 for £250. Frost was a leading figure of the St Ives School and an advocate of abstraction in Britain. In the 1950s Frost began a series of works (of which this is one) inspired by the boats he would watch in the harbour at St Ives. The intersecting lines in this work echo the shapes of the boats and their rocking motion on the waves of the sea, the curves of the ropes that secured them in the water, the arcs of their swaying masts and *Boats – Argenteuil* by Manet which she had purchased in 1920.

Utrillo and Oskar Kokoshka among others. These were funded by the sale, early in 1960, of works she felt were duplicates. Otherwise the prices Margaret was paying were far less than the amounts spent on her earlier purchases, often less than a hundred pounds.

Some modern British art had been bought for the Museum's collection by David Baxandall who was Assistant Keeper, then Keeper of Art from 1928 to 1941. His taste and enthusiasm was advanced in the climate of the Welsh art scene of the day and it was under his direction that the Museum made what were considered daring purchases of work by David Jones, Gwen John, Winifred Nicholson, Henri Gaudier-Brzeska and Augustus John. After Baxandall's departure, the acquisition of work by major contemporary artists slowed until Henry Moore's *Upright Motif no. 8* was purchased in 1962. The acquisitions Margaret was making in the 1950s were therefore vital. Much of the modern British art in the national collection was bought from the 1970s onwards, and the second Davies bequest convinced the authorities of the need to develop this area. Certainly the bequest filled major gaps – several artists are still only represented in the national collection by the work Margaret bought.

Margaret's more avant-garde taste may have been due to her own painting. In her early diaries it is clear that Margaret looks at a view in painterly terms – she talks of the colours and shapes of buildings and rivers with reference to the Impressionists, and this is possibly due to her painter's eye. It could therefore be assumed that Margaret would be more open to newer forms of painting such as abstract art, which can be said to have continued the process, begun by Impressionism, of breaking down the formalities of painting. However, from her correspondence with John Steegman, her adviser in later years, it transpires that she was not enamoured of new forms of abstract painting. In a letter dated February 1961 Steegman remarks 'I know you are not in sympathy of it in its extreme forms, any more than I am myself'. However, he goes on to say 'whether one personally likes them or not, the various degrees of abstract painting do in fact represent the accepted pictorial language of our time, to-day, and will be viewed as such in the future.'

Following the advice of Steegman, arguably the most adventurous purchase made by Margaret was the abstract painting *Brown Harbour* by Terry Frost. She had purchased *Boats – Argenteuil*, by Edouard Manet in 1920 and it may have been that she was attracted to this particular Frost because of the visual associations between the two paintings. When Steegman became Margaret's adviser is not entirely certain, although it was presumably while he was Keeper of the Department of Art at the Museum from 1945 to 1952 that he became acquainted with the Davies sisters.

Steegman was acutely aware of the issues relating to public and private collections. In the same letter to Margaret in which he offered advice on abstract art, he also talks of the transmutation of the collection from 'the *private* to the *institutional* stage … the personal tastes or distastes of the collector must to some extent give way to the tastes and requirements of the art-interested public, young and old, not only of to-day but also of tomorrow'. He goes on to emphasize that her taste is still important but that she should consider buying artists' work that she would not necessarily personally favour to ensure that the collection is 'rounded off'. Interestingly, he specifically mentions Graham Sutherland and Francis Bacon, neither of whom she bought.

Margaret Davies did not always adhere exactly to her adviser's counsel. However, as Steegman also told her, 'I think a collection such as yours, destined for the public, should retain to some extent the tastes of the collector, as much in its exclusions as in its inclusions, in order to provide the personal flavour which has always been a marked feature of the major English art-collections'. It is this sense of the collector's personal taste that ensured the bequest of modern British art not only proved fundamental in expanding the national collection in sparse areas, but also served to set the seeds for future collecting, both public and private, that continues to this day.

Above: Ivon Hitchens, *Trees from a House roof: Autumn,* 1947. Bought from the Leicester Galleries in 1950 for £121 15d, this work, along with *Brown Harbour* by Frost, is one of the most abstract paintings owned by Margaret. Although it seems her taste was more avant-garde than her sister Gwendoline, she disliked extreme forms of abstraction. © *The Estate of Ivon Hitchens*

BIBLIOGRAPHY

INTRODUCTION

Campbell, Bruce A., 'The battle of the sites: a national museum for Wales', (unpublished University of Leicester Ph.D. thesis, 2006).

Dictionary of Welsh Biography and its supplements (B. H. Blackwell Ltd, 1959), for short biographies of people mentioned in this chapter.

Ellis, E. L., *The University College of Wales, Aberystwyth, 1872–1972* (University of Wales Press, 2004).

Ellis, E. L., *T. J.: a life of Dr Thomas Jones, CH* (University of Wales Press, 1992).

Ellis, T. I., *John Humphreys Davies, 1871–1926* (Liverpool, 1963).

Howell, David W., *Land and people in nineteenth-century Wales* (Studies in economic history) (Routledge and Kegan Paul, 1977).

Hughes, Glyn Tegai, Morgan, Prys and Thomas, J. Gareth (eds), *Gregynog* (University of Wales Press, 1977).

Idwal Jones, Kitty (ed.) *Syr Herbert Lewis, 1858–1933* (University of Wales Press,1958).

Jenkins, David, *A refuge in peace and war: the National Library of Wales to 1952* (National Library of Wales, 2002).

Jones, Thomas, *A diary with letters, 1931–50* (Oxford University Press, 1954).

Lord, Peter, *The visual culture of Wales: imaging the nation* (University of Wales Press, 2000).

Lord, Peter, *The visual culture of Wales: industrial society* (University of Wales Press, 1998).

Lloyd-Morgan, Ceridwen, 'Gwendoline and Margaret Davies', in *Oxford Dictionary of National Biography* (Oxford University Press, 2004).

Morgan, Kenneth O., 'David Davies, 1880–1944', in *Oxford Dictionary of National Biography* (Oxford University Press, 2004).

Morgan, Kenneth O., *Rebirth of a nation (History of Wales 1880–1980)* (Oxford University Press, 1981).

Morgan, Prys, *The University of Wales, 1939–1993* (University of Wales Press, 1997).

Parrott, Ian, *The spiritual pilgrims* (C. Davies, 1969).

Thomas, Ivor, *Top Sawyer: a biography of David Davies of Llandinam* (Longmans, 1938; reprint, Golden Grove Edition, 1988).

Thomas, Owen, *Cofiant y Parchedig John Jones, Talsarn* (Wrexham, 1874).

White, Eirene, *The Ladies of Gregynog* (University of Wales Press, 1985)

Williams, J. Gwynn, *The university movement in Wales* (University of Wales Press, 1993).

Interview

Dora Herbert Jones, 1967.

WHATSOEVER THY HAND FINDETH TO DO

Boyns, Trevor, 'Growth in the coal industry: the cases of Powell Duffryn and the Ocean Coal Company, 1864–1913', in Baber, Colin and Williams, L.J., *Modern South Wales: essays in economic history* (University of Wales Press, 1986).

Christiansen, Rex and Miller, R. W., *The Cambrian railways, Vol. 1, 1852–1888,* (David & Charles, 1967).

Jones, Goronwy, *David Davies (1818–1890), Llandinam* (Hughes, 1913). In Welsh.

Jones, Gwyn Briwnant, *Railway through Talerddig* (Gomer, 1990).

Protheroe, I. W., 'The port and railways of Barry', in Moore, Donald (ed.), *Barry: the Centenary Book* (Barry Centenary Book Committee,1984).

Tedstone, M. A., *The Barry railway steamers* (Oakwood Press, 2005).

Thomas, Ivor, *Top Sawyer: a biography of David Davies of Llandinam* (Longmans, 1938; reprint, Golden Grove, 1988).

Williams, Herbert, *Davies the Ocean: railway king and coal tycoon* (University of Wales Press, 1991).

MUCH THAT IS BEAUTIFUL

Dumas, Ann and Robins, Ann, *Cézanne in Britain* (exhibition catalogue, National Gallery, London, 2006).

Ellis-Jones, Michael, *A boyhood's recall 1937–1945*, (the author, 2006).

Evans, Mark, 'The Davies sisters of Llandinam and Impressionism for Wales, 1908–1923', *Journal of the History of Collections*, 16, no. 2, 2004.

Ingamells, John, *The Davies Collection of French art* (Amgueddfa Cymru – National Museum Wales, 1967).

McIntyre, Bethany, *Sisters Select: Works on paper from the Davies Collection* (Amgueddfa Cymru – National Museum Wales, 2000).

Meyrick, Robert, 'Hugh Blaker: doing his bit for the moderns', *Journal of the History of Collections*, 16, no. 2, 2004.

Rowan, Eric and Stewart, Carolyn, *An elusive tradition: art and society in Wales 1870–1950* (University of Wales Press, 2002).

Sumner, Ann, *Colour and Light: fifty Impressionist and Post-Impressionist works at the National Museum of Wales* (Amgueddfa Cymru – National Museum Wales, 2005).

Manuscripts (private collections)

Early journal for visit to London to celebrate Queen Victoria's Jubilee, 1897.

Autograph school book Gwendoline Davies, 1899.

Autograph school book Margaret Davies, 1902.

Notes of a lecture series given by Miss Watson in Dresden, 1907-8.

Gwendoline's art historical table of Italian artists, undated.

Gwendoline's Italian tour journal, 1909.

Margaret's Italian tour journal, 1909.

Margaret's journal of a week in Bayreuth, 1909.

Margaret's journal of a European tour in the family Daimler, 1910.

Margaret's journal of a winter in France and Southern Italy, probably 1913–14.

Translation of A. Vollard 's *Life of Cézanne* from the French, in Margaret's hand, 1918.

KNOCKED TO PIECES

Art in exile: Flanders, Wales and the First World War, (exhibition catalogue, Museum of Fine Arts, Ghent; Hannema-de Stuers Foundation, Heino; Amgueddfa Cymru – National Museum Wales, 2002).

Dixon, Agnes M., *The Cantineers* (John Murray, 1917).

Evans, Mark, 'The Davies sisters of Llandinam and Impressionism for Wales, 1908–1923', *Journal of the History of Collections*, 16, no. 2, 2004.

Evans, Mark and Fairclough, Oliver, *The National Museum of Wales: A companion guide to the National Art Gallery* (Amgueddfa Cymru – National Museum Wales, 1993).

Lord, Peter, *The Visual Culture of Wales: imaging the Nation* (University of Wales Press, 2000).

Rowan, Eric and Stewart, Carolyn, *An elusive tradition: art and society in Wales, 1870-1950* (University of Wales Press, 2002).

Vincentelli, Moira, 'The Davies family and Belgian refugee artists and musicians in Wales', *National Library of Wales Journal*, XXII, 1981.

White, Eirene, *The Ladies of Gregynog* (University of Wales Press, 1985).

Manuscripts (private collections)

Margaret's journals 1917 and 1918; essays on canteen life, album of photographs, autographs, etc.

Gwendoline's album of photographs, autographs etc.

Manuscripts (public collections)

Thomas Jones papers, National Library of Wales; Davies collection archive, National Museum of Wales; Papers of Mrs E. J. Rideal and Mrs L. C. Cowper, Imperial War Museum.

THE BEAUTY OF SIMPLICITY

Holland, Neil and Meyrick, Robert, *To instruct and inspire: 125 years of the Arts and Crafts collection* (University of Wales Press, 1997).

Hughes, Glyn Tegai, Morgan, Prys and Thomas, J. Gareth (eds), *Gregynog* (University of Wales Press, 1977).

Shen, Lindsay, 'Philanthropic furnishing: Gregynog Hall, Powys', *Furniture History,* 31 (1995).

Vincentelli, Moira, '*The U.C.W. Arts and Crafts Museum*', Ceredigion, Journal of the Ceredigion Antiquarian Society, 9, no.1, 1980.

White, Eirene, *The Ladies of Gregynog* (University of Wales Press, 1985).

Manuscripts (public collections)

Thomas Jones papers, National Library of Wales, University of Wales and Gregynog.

WEALTH WISE AND CULTURE KIND

Ellis, E. L., T. J.: *A Life of Dr Thomas Jones, CH* (University of Wales Press, 1992).

Grenfell, Joyce, *Joyce Grenfell requests the pleasure* (Macmillan, 1976).

Hughes, Glyn Tegai, Morgan, Prys and Thomas, J. Gareth (eds), *Gregynog* (University of Wales Press, 1977).

Jones, Thomas, *Welsh broth* (Griffiths & Co.,1951).

Jones, Thomas, *A diary with letters 1931-1950* (Oxford University Press, 1954).
White, Eirene, *The Ladies of Gregynog* (University of Wales Press, 1985).

Manuscripts (public collections)

Gregynog Hall Visitors Book 1921-1962 and *Gregynog Press Visitors Book 1923-1962* (National Library of Wales, Aberystwyth).

John Christopher, 'Gregynog reminiscences and dramatis personae', letter to Amgueddfa Cymru – National Museum Wales, 2006.

Mary Hackett, letters home 24 and 31 July 1938 (copies), Amgueddfa Cymru – National Museum Wales.

Thomas Jones, papers at the National Library of Wales.

FLINGING SONGS ACROSS THE ETHER

Allsobrook, David Ian, *Music for Wales* (University of Wales Press, 1992).

Crossley-Holland, Peter, (ed.), *Music in Wales* (Hinrichsen Edition, 1948).

Davies, Henry Walford, The musical outlook in Wales *(Welsh Outlook,* 1926).

Gibbs, Alan, 'Gustav Holst and Gregynog' in *Transactions of the Honourable Society of Cymmrodorion 2003*, Vol. 10, 2004.

Hywel, John, 'Music during the Davies Period' in Hughes, Glyn Tegai, Morgan, Prys and Thomas

J. Gareth, (eds), *Gregynog* (University of Wales Press, 1977).

Parrott, Ian, 'Warlock in Wales', *The Musical Times,* Vol. 105, no. 1460, 1964.

Parrott, Ian, *The spiritual pilgrims* (C. Davies, 1969).

Various National Council of Music publications, 1920-22

Manuscripts (private collections)

Margaret Davies's Bayreuth journals, August 1909 and August 1911.

Manuscripts (public collections)

Walford Davies Archive, Royal College of Music, London; University of Wales Department of Music archive; Welsh Folk-Song Society archive; Gwendoline Davies letters to Thomas Jones, Lucie Barbier, all National Library of Wales.

THE GAIETY OF THESE BOOKS

Bakker, Steven A., *The Miss Margaret Sidney Davies complete collection of special Gregynog bindings* (De Zilverdistel N. V. Rare Books, Antwerp, 1995).

Davies, J. Michael, *The private press at Gregynog* (Leicester College of Art, 1959).

Ellis, E. L. *T. J.: a life of Dr Thomas Jones, CH* (University of Wales Press, 1992).

Fish, Wendy, *Gregynog Press: illustrated from material in the National Art Library* (Victoria and Albert Museum, London, 1987).

Haberly, Loyd, *An American book-builder in England and Wales: reminiscences of the Seven Acres and Gregynog presses* (Bertram Rota, 1979).

Harrop, Dorothy A., 'George Fisher and the Gregynog Press', *The Book Collector*, 19/4, 1970.

Harrop, Dorothy A., *A history of the Gregynog Press* (Private Libraries Association, Pinner, 1980).

Hodgson, H., *Herbert Hodgson, printer; work for T. E. Lawrence and at Gregynog* (The Fleece Press, 1989).

Hughes, Glyn Tegai, Morgan, Prys and Thomas, J. Gareth (eds), *Gregynog* (University of Wales Press, 1977).

Hughes-Stanton, Penelope, *The wood engravings of Blair Hughes-Stanton* (Private Libraries Association, Pinner, 1991).

Hutchins, Michael, *Printing at Gregynog/Argraffu yng Ngregynog* (Welsh Arts Council, 1976).

Jones, Thomas, *A diary with letters 1931–1950* (Oxford University Press, 1954).

Jones, Thomas, *The Gregynog Press: a paper read to the Double Crown Club on 7 April 1954* (Oxford University Press, 1954).

Rogerson, Ian, *Agnes Miller Parker: wood engravings from 'Fables of Esope'* (Gwasg Gregynog, 1996).

Rogerson, Ian, *Agnes Miller Parker: wood engravings from ' XXI Welsh gypsy folk-tales'* (Gwasg Gregynog, 1997).

Rogerson, Ian, *The wood engravings of Agnes Miller Parker* (The British Library, 2005).

Selborne, Joanna, *British wood-engraved book illustration 1904-1940* (Clarendon Press, 1998).

White, Eirene, *The Ladies of Gregynog* (University of Wales Press, 1985).

AN ALL-CONSUMING DRIVE

Dawkes, Bryony and Meyrick, Robert, *Radical visions: British Art 1910-1950* (Oriel Davies Gallery, Newtown, 2006).

Elsner, John and Cardinal, Roger, *Cultures of collecting* (Reaktion Books, 1994).

Evans, Mark and Fairclough, Oliver, *The National Museum of Wales: A companion guide to the National Art Gallery* (Amgueddfa Cymru – National Museum Wales, 1993).

Ingamells, John, 'The Margaret Davies Bequest to the National Museum of Wales', *The Connoisseur*, 156, 1964.

McIntyre, Bethany, *Sisters Select: works on paper from the Davies collection* (Amgueddfa Cymru – National Museum Wales, 2000).

Rollo, Charles, *Catalogue of the Margaret S. Davies Bequest of Paintings, Drawings and Sculpture* (Amgueddfa Cymru – National Museum Wales, 1963).

Rowan, Eric and Stewart, Carolyn, *An elusive tradition: art and society in Wales 1870–1950* (University of Wales Press, 2002).

Sumner, Ann, *Colour and Light: fifty Impressionist and Post-Impressionist works at the National Museum of Wales* (Amgueddfa Cymru – National Museum Wales, 2005).

Wilson, Simon, *Tate Gallery: An illustrated companion* (Tate Gallery Publications, 1995).

NOTES ON CONTRIBUTORS

Prof. Prys Morgan is Emeritus Professor of History at the University of Wales, Swansea.

Robert Meyrick is Head of the School of Art and Keeper of Art at the University of Wales, Aberystwyth.

At Amgueddfa Cymru – National Museum Wales:

Louisa Briggs is Curator of Modern & Contemporary Art, Bryony Dawkes is Curator of Celf Cymru Gyfan - Artshare Wales, one of Amgueddfa Cymru's formal partnership projects, Oliver Fairclough is Keeper of Art, Eveline Holsappel is Assistant Curator of Applied Art, Dr David Jenkins is Senior Curator of Industry, John Kenyon is Librarian and Dr Ann Sumner is Head of Fine Art.

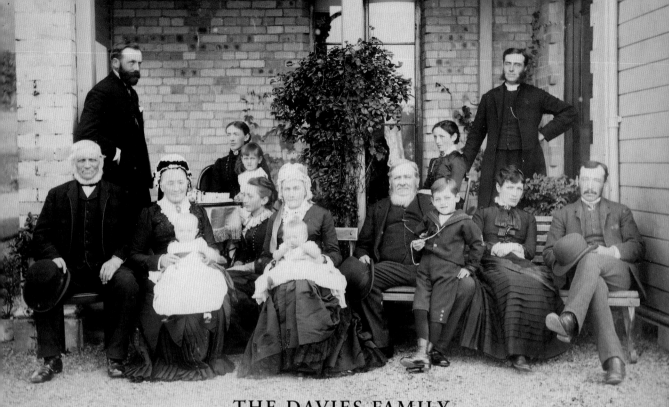

THE DAVIES FAMILY

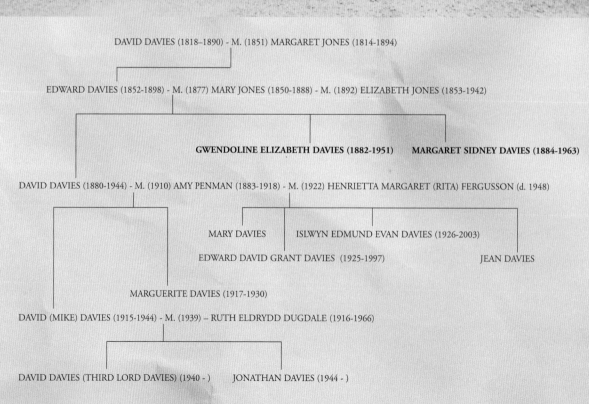

DAVID DAVIES (1818–1890) - M. (1851) MARGARET JONES (1814-1894)

EDWARD DAVIES (1852-1898) - M. (1877) MARY JONES (1850-1888) - M. (1892) ELIZABETH JONES (1853-1942)

GWENDOLINE ELIZABETH DAVIES (1882-1951)   **MARGARET SIDNEY DAVIES (1884-1963)**

DAVID DAVIES (1880-1944) - M. (1910) AMY PENMAN (1883-1918) - M. (1922) HENRIETTA MARGARET (RITA) FERGUSSON (d. 1948)

MARY DAVIES   ISLWYN EDMUND EVAN DAVIES (1926-2003)

EDWARD DAVID GRANT DAVIES (1925-1997)   JEAN DAVIES

MARGUERITE DAVIES (1917-1930)

DAVID (MIKE) DAVIES (1915-1944) - M. (1939) – RUTH ELDRYDD DUGDALE (1916-1966)

DAVID DAVIES (THIRD LORD DAVIES) (1940 -)   JONATHAN DAVIES (1944 -)